Mini-lessons
for
Literature Circles

Mini-lessons for Literature Circles

Harvey Daniels
Nancy Steineke

Heinemann
Portsmouth, NH

Heinemann
A division of Reed Elsevier Inc.
361 Hanover Street
Portsmouth, NH 03801–3912
www.heinemann.com

Offices and agents throughout the world

The authors and publisher wish to thank those who have generously given permission to reprint borrowed material:

"Offender/Victim Comparison." Copyright © 2003 by the Chicago Tribune Company. All rights reserved. Used by permission.

"Students Face Discipline in Hazing Case" by Lisa Black. Copyright © 2003 by the Chicago Tribune Company. All rights reserved. Used by permission.

Library of Congress Cataloging-in-Publication Data
Daniels, Harvey, 1947–
    Mini-lessons for literature circles / Harvey Daniels, Nancy Steineke.
        p.   cm.
    ISBN 0-325-00702-0 (alk. paper)
    1. Group reading.   2. Book clubs (Discussion groups).   3. Literature—Study and teaching.   4. Children—Books and reading.   I. Steineke, Nancy.
II. Title.
LC6631.D38   2004
372.41'62—dc22   2004009666

Editor: Leigh Peake
Production management: Sarah Weaver
Production coordination: Abigail M. Heim
Typesetter: Technologies 'N Typography
Interior design: Joyce Weston Design
Cover design: Catherine Hawkes, Cat & Mouse
Manufacturing: Louise Richardson

Printed in the United States of America on acid-free paper
08 07 06   RRD   5

Contents

10 Do It Yourself! 277

Appendix 281

Acknowledgments

Whenever you write a book about teaching, the main people you need to thank are your students. Between the two of us, we have (yikes!) sixty-two years of teaching experience, and every student we have taught is in here somewhere. Without knowing those several thousand young people, we'd never have the knowledge, the stories, the materials, the lessons, the pictures that make up this book.

Next, we want to thank all those teachers who have welcomed us into their classrooms, talked to us at conferences, attended our summer workshops, or emailed us about their literature circle problems and breakthroughs. This book grew directly out of those colleagues' questions and suggestions. Many thanks to the four schools where many of the lessons in this book were refined: Victor J. Andrew High School in Tinley Park, IL; Best Practice High School in Chicago; Baker Demonstration School in Evanston, IL; and Federal-Hocking High School in Stewart, OH. We especially want to thank the teachers who handed over their kids for our mad-scientist experiments. Thanks for letting us cook in your kitchens.

Smokey wants to acknowledge his far-flung personal book club. Elaine, the mother of all readers, somehow manages to fit fifty books a year around her university duties, doling out her top recommendations to the rest of us. Marny is an artist in Santa Fe whose tastes run to contemporary fiction, with a special fondness for Pat Conroy. Nick, a pathologist's assistant in Minnesota, mixes business with pleasure, ranging widely across the fields of pathology, forensics, and crime investigation. Maybe the family that reads together doesn't stay *physically* together, but books bind the Daniels wherever we go.

Nancy wants to acknowledge her husband Bill. Besides designing and building a most fabulous third-floor attic office that removes her from all of the distractions the rest of the house has to offer, Bill is THE MAN when it comes to the use of a highlighter. She always lets Bill have the first crack at the *Chicago Tribune* and *Newsweek* because he highlights all the good articles. For example, did you catch the one about the guy who is digging up his farm in Minnesota searching for caves? See, if Bill were around you wouldn't have missed that one! However, Nancy's biggest debt to Bill is that he puts up with her; you'd think he'd get an award for that, but so far it's only led to two book acknowledgments and twenty-five anniversaries.

Much of this book was written longhand on cross-country plane trips, yielding an output of virtually indecipherable text. Thanks to freelance cryptographer Diane Kessler for breaking the code and magically emailing us clean copy.

Between the two of us, we have published six books with Heinemann. Hey, who wouldn't stick with an organization that's both talented and fun-loving in every department? Thanks once again to Leigh Peake, editor and horsewoman supreme; Lisa Luedeke, creator of a magnificent secondary list; Sarah Weaver, who shaped a very complex manuscript and taught us how to "track changes"; Abby Heim, whose design skills yield such attractive and readable books; Pat Carls, who really knows where to find readers; Eric Chalek, who sometimes succeeds at keeping us organized; Maura Sullivan, sage, seer, prognosticator and freelance guru; to Cherie Bartlett and Tracy Heine for handling our workshop road trips; and finally, to the redoubtable Lesa Scott, a principled leader who makes the whole thing work.

Mini-lessons
for
Literature Circles

Joining the Book Club

What would you say if someone asked: "What's your number one goal for your students?" If you are like us (and about a million other teachers), you might answer: "I just want my kids to become lifelong readers."

Could there be a more admirable teacherly dream? After all, if our ex-students, the young people we eventually send off into the grown-up world, are both able and eager to read, they're going to have much richer lives as citizens, workers, and parents. And since those graduates will also grow up to be our neighbors, they can help us create a community (hey, maybe even a whole country) of thoughtful, informed, and caring people.

But if we turn and look at our classrooms with this noble vision in mind, we have to wonder, "What am I really doing to nurture such lifelong readers?" Or more sternly, we might ask ourselves, "If someone came into my room today, would they see my students doing the things real readers do? What activities, what interactions am I promoting that truly invite kids into the world of books, writers, and ideas? What am I doing to build enduring, wide-ranging, critical, and self-initiated reading?"

We all realize that Friday quizzes, end-of-chapter study questions, and factual recall worksheets (or their computer-aided analogues) don't exactly kindle lifelong enchantment. No, falling in love with books means something more dynamic, something more personal, where kids are the doers, not the done-tos. So what do we do instead?

If we look at the habits of the thoughtful and curious adult readers who are our models, we see some key patterns. First, lifelong learners choose what they will read, whether fiction or nonfiction, books or articles, magazines or websites. They connect personally with the material they have chosen. They draw on a repertoire of cognitive strategies or "mind moves" to understand tough text. They often use informal kinds of writing—notes, jottings, or drawings—to deepen their understanding. After reading something significant, they often seek out other readers to talk with. Over time, they develop their own tastes, favorite authors, topics of expertise. They abandon books or articles that don't interest them and move on to something else. And they make strong judgments about the value of what they read, the artistry of authors, and the personal significance of a text. In short, they *own* reading.

This doesn't sound much like the way reading happens in school, does it? In many classrooms, the great majority of reading material is teacher-selected, with the same text assigned to everyone, regardless of interest or difficulty. The teacher's preferences—or the school district's curriculum guide—become the ruling taste. Reading is usually assigned as silent, solitary work, and rarely includes open-ended, reader-to-reader talk. Writing comes into play not as a tool for thinking but as a way of policing homework or testing recall. In short, kids in school hardly ever *own* reading the way those grown-up readers do.

Now, we're not here to grump about traditional reading instruction. Many teachers believe in a "balanced" program and feel that experiences like reading the same book as a whole class can provide a valuable shared experience. While we surely wouldn't argue with that, we still think the curriculum is drastically overbalanced with teacher-centered structures. Very few of our routine classroom activities build the habits of choice, independence, resourcefulness, and personal investment that characterize the reading lives of empowered and literate citizens.

Really Reading in Literature Circles

So, as teachers who are trying to raise real readers, how can we more fully deliver on our commitment? Tens of thousands of teachers, from kindergarten through college, are now setting aside a regular portion of the week, the month, and the whole school year for genuine "lifelong reader" experiences. These activities are not hybrids or compromises, but chunks of time that embody all the habits of true grown-up reading. And the most popular structure for delivering such experience is the literature circle or book club. Thanks to these committed teachers, today *millions* of American students are doing what real readers do, joining small, peer-led book discussion groups.

These groups are closely patterned after adult reading groups, those circles of friends who meet regularly in each other's living rooms, in church basements, or in the back rooms of bookstores to discuss a book they have chosen and read. Such book clubs have recently experienced quite a rebirth, sparked partly (and perhaps ironically) by television's *Oprah Winfrey Show,* the *Today Show,* and other programs that promote reading as well as TV-watching. Some estimates say that the number of reading groups in America has doubled since Oprah started her first book club in 1996.

What happens when we translate this simple literacy practice of adult reading groups to the educational setting? In school, we define literature circles (interchangeably called book clubs or reading groups) as small, peer-led discussion groups whose members have chosen to read the same article, poem, book, or novel and to talk about it with each other. These groups can be organized in a variety of ways, but we try to stay close to the adult reading group model. These are the consistent elements:

- Students choose their own reading materials.

- Small groups (three to six students) are formed, based upon book choice.

- Grouping is by text choices, not by "ability" or other tracking.

- Different groups choose and read different books.

- Groups create and meet on a regular schedule.

- Members write notes that help guide both their reading and their discussion.

- Discussion questions come from the students, not teachers or textbooks.

- Teacher-led mini-lessons serve as bookends, before and after meetings.

- The teacher does not lead any group, but acts as a facilitator, fellow reader, and observer.

- Personal responses, connections, and questions are the starting point of discussion.

- A spirit of playfulness and sharing pervades the room.

- When books are finished, groups share highlights of their reading with classmates through presentations, reviews, dramatizations, book chats, or other activities.

- New groups form around new reading choices, and another cycle begins.

- Assessment is by teacher observation and student self-evaluation.

What Do Book Clubs Look Like?

That was a list of ingredients; now here's a picture. If you walk into a classroom where literature circles are meeting, you'll see maybe five or six groups of students gathered at tables or in tight clusters of desks, talking quietly. As you walk past, you'll notice that each group is reading a different text, and every student has brought some kind of writing (a journal, some sticky notes, an annotated bookmark) to remind them of points they want to raise with their friends. If you listen in on some discussions, you'll find that the conversations are "leaderless," meaning that every member has personal responsibility for contributing to a lively, productive, and on-track discussion.

In smoothly functioning groups, students take turns, share airtime, introduce meaty topics, follow up on each other's ideas, and consistently anchor their comments in specific passages of the text. The conversation is free-flowing, spontaneous, back-and-forth, and natural. The young readers assert, question, hypothesize, argue, pause, ponder, and laugh. The activity looks, and is, enjoyable. In classrooms where teachers have implemented book clubs, students often call it their favorite part of the day.

And what is the teacher doing while all the students talk books? You'll see the teacher roaming from group to group, sitting in briefly, perhaps making some notes, but talking very little and definitely not running the discussions. If you come early and stay late, you'll notice that the literature circle session actually has three steps: a brief introductory mini-lesson led by the teacher; a long chunk of meeting time for the students, during which the teacher monitors and assists; and another short mini-lesson or debriefing session conducted by the teacher at the end. Typically, these discussions happen one to three times a week, with students using the "off days" to read ahead in their books and make notes for the next discussion. The teacher may also use those alternate days to provide mini-lessons aimed at improving the next round of meetings. The design and delivery of these opening and closing mini-lessons are the main subject of this book.

Is that enough background? We probably don't have to sell you on the value of literature circles. If you picked up this book, you're either thinking seriously about starting book clubs in your classroom or you already have, and you're looking for ways to refine them, to deepen kids' conversations, and to explore new variations. And that's just what this book is about: using quick and powerful mini-lessons, just before and just after kids' small-group meetings, to enhance the social interactions, sharpen the focus, solve predictable problems, and steer students toward deeper literary appreciation and lifetime reading habits. If you are concerned about the broader issues, such as what research has to say about lit circles or how book clubs can help us meet educational standards, just hang on until the end of this chapter and we'll fill you in.

What Are Mini-lessons?

Mini-lessons are short, focused, teacher-directed activities used before and after each meeting of literature circles, book clubs, or any student-centered reading discussions. This book offers forty-five such lessons, designed to be used with students from sixth grade through high school who are at all stages of book club development, from brand-new beginners to grizzled old-timers.

Our colleague Nancie Atwell (1998, 150) has shown how lessons like these differ from traditional teacher presentations:

> The mini-lesson is a forum for my authority—the things *I* know that will help writers and readers grow. I have experiences as an adult that my students have not had, and it's my responsibility to share the knowledge I do have—and seek the knowledge that I don't—that will help them move forward. The mini-lesson is also a forum for students to share what *they* know and for us to figure out collaboratively what we know, to think and produce knowledge together and lay claim to it as a community. It's an occasion for establishing a communal frame of reference, for us to develop vocabulary, criteria and procedures together.

The majority of mini-lessons in this book are genuinely "mini" in length. Five to fifteen minutes is often enough time to introduce a single skill, to practice a new strategy, or to demonstrate a helpful variation. But we also share a few twenty- and thirty-minute lessons; they take longer because they include practice time using real literature, not because the teacher talks more. Along with Atwell, we have begun "seeing some mini-lessons as *long*— twenty minutes—and *interactive:* teachers and students working together" (p. 151). We surpass even Atwell's generous maximum duration a couple of times, but we hold steadfastly to this rule: These are mini-*lessons,* not mini-lectures.

Why Do You Need Mini-lessons?

Literature circles are a fun but relatively complex activity. When we introduce them to the classroom, we need to provide a period of initial training, especially if collaborative small-group work is unfamiliar or difficult for the students. During that first phase of preparation, we try to ensure that kids have enough social, cognitive, and literary skills to begin functioning in peer-led book talk groups.

But the initial training is never enough: Problems crop up, discussions wander, logistics fail, personalities clash, schedules conflict, books disappoint, kids forget their notes. So we need an ongoing, systematic structure for shaping, refining, and extending that initial training. This steady refinement is especially important since literature circles, once established, can continue all year long, cycle after cycle, becoming a major, recurrent fixture of the classroom. It is definitely worth the investment of time to persistently steer students toward deeper discussions, smoother social processes, and more sophisticated literary insight.

What Topics Do Mini-lessons Cover?

Mini-lessons involve three major, overlapping topics:

- the social skills necessary for effective small-group discussion
- the cognitive strategies that help readers to understand texts
- the literary lenses smart readers use to examine and appreciate what they read

These three topics are intertwined throughout this book; they come up in every chapter. Many of the individual mini-lessons address social skills, reading strategies, and literary appreciation all at once.

....

Social Skills

Kids need sufficient social skills to operate as effective members of a small, collaborative work group. Now, we can hear you thinking: "I've got some real doozies in my class. I've got kids who couldn't collaborate with their own shadow—not to mention four other students." We know, we know. We've got six decades of teaching experience under our collective belt and we've met plenty of doozies and doozettes ourselves. But that's really the point: No one is born with good collaborative skills—you have to learn them. And hey, we're teachers—isn't that handy? We can teach kids the social skills they need.

So what is the specific inventory of social skills needed in a book club? One of Harvey's classes developed this list:

take turns

listen actively

make eye contact

lean forward

nod, confirm, respond

share airtime

include everybody

don't dominate

pull other people in

don't interrupt

speak directly to each other

receive others' ideas

be tolerant

honor people's "burning issues"

piggyback on ideas of others

speak up when you disagree

respect differences

disagree constructively

don't attack

stay focused, on task

support your views with the book

trust each other

be responsible to the group

No, you don't need students who possess all these skills. (Who does? What adult book club members would score 100 on this checklist?) What you need are kids who have enough social facility to begin working in a small discussion group.

If we put aside our teacher skepticism for a moment, we will realize that our eleven- or fourteen- or eighteen-year-old students actually do possess many of these social skills. Every day, we see them taking turns, making excellent eye contact, raising rich topics, and asking cogent follow-up questions— when they talk among themselves about movies, clothes, video games, or this week's un-favorite teacher. So, a big part of our job is tapping into skills that students have already mastered in nonclassroom contexts, and importing them into the curriculum. Still, of course, much of the work involves introducing skills (such as disagreeing respectfully) that students may not yet have developed. Accordingly, lots of mini-lessons in this book deal with both the development and the maintenance of social skills needed to be a reliable and collaborative book club member.

Reading Strategies

For book clubs (or any reading activity) to succeed, kids need to understand and remember what they read. And that's not necessarily a slam-dunk. When literature circles started to get popular ten and fifteen years ago, our understanding of reading-as-thinking was at a pretty early stage, and few teachers were showing kids the specific cognitive moves that skilled readers use to crack tough texts. Today, things have really changed, thanks to the wonderful work of Keene and Zimmerman (1997), Harvey and Goudvis (2000), and others. Now we can explain to our students that smart readers:

Visualize—they make mental pictures or sensory images as they read.

Connect—they connect the text to their own experience, to events in the world, to other readings.

Question—they actively wonder, surface uncertainties, and interrogate the text, the author, or the characters.

Infer—they predict, hypothesize, interpret, and draw conclusions.

Evaluate—they determine relative importance, make judgments, develop critiques.

Analyze—they notice elements of the author's craft: text structures, language, style, theme, point of view.

Recall—they can retell, summarize, and remember information.

Self-monitor—they can recognize and act upon uncertainty as they read; adjusting, troubleshooting, fixing up their understanding.

Because these thinking strategies are so vital to solid comprehension and lively conversation, many teachers now explicitly teach this thinking repertoire as basic equipment for any language arts course. All of Chapter 3 and many other mini-lessons throughout the book show kids how to put these strategies to work in their literature circle meetings.

Literary Analysis

Our third topic for mini-lessons is a slightly tricky one. Obviously, we want our students, whether they are sixth graders first venturing into young adult (YA) literature or high school seniors reading adult novels, to increasingly notice and think about literary structures, styles, and conventions. After all, those lifelong readers that we want our students to become can, among other things, analyze a book's structure. Formal literary analysis helps us, both kid and adult alike, to understand how books get built and to enter into an ever-broader range of conversations with fellow readers. Such study also feeds our own writing; it teaches us to read like a writer, thinking about the tools an author chooses and uses. For these and other good reasons, we feature five such literary mini-lessons in Chapter 7 (and others scattered through the book) that focus on the craft of authorship.

But we also subscribe to "reader response theory," as originated by Louise Rosenblatt (1996) and interpreted by Robert Probst (2004). This school of thought says, among many other smart things, that response must precede analysis; that readers have to connect personally to a book before they can study it, dissect it, appraise its components. Indeed, reader response theory holds that "literature" is actually a co-creation of the reader and the author, distinct and unique upon each reading. One implication of reader response theory for schooling is that you should not try to reverse the order, marching students through a word-by-word, page-by-page analysis of a book, and expect them to connect personally with the text later on. Literature has to work first as a story that speaks to the whole human reader before it can be studied as an external work of art.

Of course, what we have just described is exactly the way literature was taught to us when we were in high school—and how it often gets taught today. Sometimes, we teachers *do* march kids through our personal list of hidden symbols, obscure metaphors, subtle turning points, clever language, deft plot structures, and "correct" interpretations. The idea that *analyzing* is the proper way to approach literature is alive and very well in America's secondary schools. The still-dominant school of New Criticism holds that the right answers are lodged in the text, and certainly not co-created by any reader.

We're not trying to start an all-or-nothing debate here. It's fine with us if you want to assign *To Kill a Mockingbird* and provide the kids with your personal concordance of interpretations and structural insights. Harvey well remembers the college professor who gave two whole class periods to "explicating" the first paragraph of Vladimir Nabokov's *Lolita*. It was a fabulously entertaining tour of the professor's psyche, mostly unrelated to the book, but it sure did spark careful reading and discussion among the students. So there's nothing wrong with kids watching a veteran reader dissect a book she admires profoundly and understands deeply. Heck, we might do the same thing next semester with *The Things They Carried*. But we wouldn't do *only* that, book after book. It's all about balance. Right now, too many school days are filled with teacher-driven activities focused exclusively on literary analysis. That type of teaching doesn't engage all kids all the time, and it's not the way most lifelong readers think. So we need to make room for other approaches to books.

When Do You Teach Mini-lessons?

Successful teachers use a wide array of scheduling patterns, and we're going to show you two alternatives. In the first version, what you might call the "streamlined" model, literature circles use just two class periods a week, and the other three days are saved for other activities. In this schedule, the teacher might divide two fifty-minute literature circle days into three parts:

5–15 minutes: introductory mini-lesson

20–30 minutes: small-group meeting time

5–15 minutes: sharing time or closing mini-lesson

Many teachers allow two to four weeks for student groups to read and discuss a book, and have literature circles meet three to six times during this period. On club meeting days, teachers offer targeted mini-lessons at strategic times: just before kids meet in their peer-led groups, or immediately afterwards, or both. If students need help selecting books at the beginning, that's a good time for a book-picking mini-lesson; if they are midbook and struggling with unbalanced group member contributions, a mini-lesson on sharing airtime might be timely. Calendar 1 shows a cycle of book club meetings built around this pattern, including sample mini-lesson topics highlighted in bold type.

Several assumptions are built into this calendar, none of which are sacred or correct. (In a minute we'll show you a very different approach.)

- All class periods are forty-five minutes.
- Two or three days a week will be used for literature circle activities.
- Much of the reading will be done outside of class.
- Class time will be used only for mini-lessons, meetings, and sharing.
- Two and a half weeks is long enough to read the book.
- Four meetings along the way is just right.

This is a favorite calendar of teachers who have lots of other curriculum demands, and have limited class time to devote to book clubs.

Calendar 2 is the schedule Nancy recently used for the first-ever literature circle cycle with one sophomore group. Although this timetable looks complicated, she's simply using part of *every* class period to support the book clubs, while Calendar 1 crams all of the literature circle activities into two days a week. Nancy's schedule shows four small-group meetings over a one-month period, supported by twelve mini-lessons. Like the other calendar, this one has some built-in assumptions.

Calendar 1

Monday	Tuesday	Wednesday	Thursday	Friday
	• Hand out books • **Making a Schedule (10)** • **Bookmarks (10)** • Reading time (25) • Debrief first chapter (10)	• Homework: Reading and notes	• Homework: Reading and notes	• **Savoring Powerful Language (15)** • *Meeting #1* (25) • Debrief (5)
• Homework: Reading and notes	• **Sharing Airtime (10)** • *Meeting #2* (25) • Debrief (10)	• Homework: Reading and notes	• Homework: Reading and notes	• **Follow-up Questions (10)** • *Meeting #3* (25) • Debrief (10)
• Homework: Reading and notes	• **Readers Theater (10)** • *Meeting #4* (25) • Debrief (10)	• **More Readers Theater (10)** • Work time (35)	• Readers Theater Performances (45)	

Bold items are mini-lessons.
Numbers in parentheses indicate minutes.

WHEN DO YOU TEACH MINI-LESSONS? ■ 13

- The schedule is based on a fifty-minute period.

- Book discussion meetings occur once a week, usually on Fridays.

- Four weeks are needed since some groups are reading really long books.

- Almost every class period, five days a week, has some time devoted to lit circle activities.

- Except for meeting days, the class always begins with fifteen minutes for silent reading.

- All of the mini-lessons are presented on nondiscussion days.

- Mini-lessons aimed at discussion improvement take place the day before a meeting.

- The mini-lesson for improving questions is on a Monday with the hopes that students will use that mini-lesson as they prepare for Friday's discussion.

- Mini-lessons for introducing students to various performance projects are presented in the first and second week so that students can make educated project choices and begin planning during the third meeting.

- Cover curriculum means just that. Nancy still has to address all the other curricular requirements of her department.

We think that a schedule like Nancy's works better for beginners because it provides much more student support and allocates parts of all five days for reading, writing, and mini-lessons. When students are new to book clubs, working on literature circles every day keeps the books and groups in the front of student consciousness. Some teachers begin the year with Nancy's model, then shift to Calendar 1 later in the term when their students have learned the ropes and don't need as much in-class support.

How many mini-lessons does it take to effectively support student-led book clubs? Or, to put it another way, how much can students absorb, practice, and learn? In Calendar 2, you'll notice that each book club meeting is preceded by as many as three mini-lessons over a couple of days. In the "streamlined" model, there's usually just one mini-lesson before each meeting, with sharing and debriefing time afterward. This shows the range of choices teachers make, depending on the needs of their students, the

Calendar 2

Monday	Tuesday	Wednesday	Thursday	Friday
• Hand out books (10) • Read 20 minutes (20) • **Written Conversation (10)** • Discuss beginning of book in group (5) • **Membership Grid (5)**	• **Membership Grid (5)** • **Develop Reading Schedule (10)** • **Determine Liability Policy (5)** • Read remainder of period	• SSR (20) • **Tableaux Demo (30)**	• SSR (15) • **T-Chart: Friendliness and Support (10)** • Cover curriculum (25)	• *Meeting #1* • **Membership Grid (5)** • Discussion (25) • Processing/debriefing (10) • Journal reflection (10)
• SSR (20) • **Readers Theater Demo (30)**	• SSR (15) • **The Envelope, Please (10)** • Cover curriculum (25)	• SSR (15) • **Talk Show Demo (15)** • **Membership Grid (5)** • Group meeting: Discuss project ideas, compare reading progress to calendar (10) • Large-group project discussion (5)	• **Save the Last Word for Me (20)** • Cover curriculum (30) or read remainder of period	• *Meeting #2* • **Membership Grid (5)** • Discussion (25) • Project brainstorm (10) • Processing/debriefing (10) • Journal reflection—homework
• SSR (15) • **Improving Discussion Questions (15)** • Cover curriculum (20)	• SSR (15) • Cover curriculum (35)	• SSR (15) • Cover curriculum (35)	• SSR (15) • Review project options (5) • Show old class video examples and sample scripts (30)	• *Meeting #3* • **Membership Grid (5)** • Discussion (25) • Project planning (15) • Processing/debriefing (5) • Journal reflection—homework
• SSR (15) • Cover curriculum (35)	• SSR (15) • **Improving Save the Last Word and Using Friendliness & Support (35)**	• *Meeting #4* • **Membership Grid (5)** • Discussion (25) • Finish project planning (15) • Processing/debriefing (5) • Journal reflection—homework	• Cover curriculum (30) • Practice performances (20)	• Project performances

Bold items are mini-lessons.
Numbers in parentheses indicate minutes.

difficulty of the books, the demands of their curriculum, and a dozen other on-the-ground factors.

Do Literature Circles Run All Year Long?

Looking at these two calendars, you might be wondering: What goes on the other eight months of the year? Do you have literature circles running all the time, one cycle after another? You won't be surprised to hear us say that yes, we think book clubs should continue all year long, just like adult reading groups. One of the wonderful features of literature circles is that they can recur indefinitely, without extensive planning by the teacher. Once kids have learned the rules, all you need is new books (and a few mini-lessons) to keep book clubs going throughout the year. Plus, it seems a shame to train kids for such high-level work and then use those skills only sparingly.

However, we also know that teachers face time constraints and curriculum mandates that can squeeze out even the most valuable literacy activities. And some teachers, including Nancy, prefer to spend fall semester on other collaborative literacy activities that prepare kids for full-fledged literature circles (Steineke 2002). So, to accommodate school realities and their own professional goals, many teachers run *cycles* of literature circles that alternate with other activities. For example, they'll have a round of lit circles in September and then "mothball" the activity for awhile. Maybe they'll use the time slot for a thematic unit, a whole-class novel, or some cramming for the statewide test. Then, weeks or months later, they bring literature circles back for another cycle.

In other words, you could fit anywhere from one to ten book club cycles in a school year. We think more is better, but only you know what's possible in your classroom. What we consider nonnegotiable is this: Kids must be doing some kind of independent reading all year long, whether individually or in small groups. At the least, they should have a period of sustained silent reading (SSR) every day. Preferably, when no book clubs are meeting, students should be in a true reading workshop, following the Nancie Atwell model. That means everyone is reading individually chosen books and joining in regular written conversations with classmates and conferences with the teacher.

Which Mini-lesson Do You Teach When?

We've organized our forty-five lessons in a kind of chronological order, starting with the earliest getting-organized tasks and moving on to the most refined after-book performances. This is a very general progression; you'd certainly never teach all these lessons or use them in this exact order. If you are starting new book clubs, you might draw one or two lessons from each chapter to help you lead students through the process. If you have been doing literature circles for a while and want to address specific problems, improve discussion skills, or spice things up with a few variations, you can jump in anywhere. But if you want to know exactly which lesson to use when, we can't tell you. You have to study your students and ask: *What's the next step for them?*

Here's the sequence of the book. The starting point, the *sine qua non* of student-centered activities like literature circles, is a collaborative classroom climate. So, in Chapter 2, we start right out with six lessons on creating an atmosphere of trust, responsibility, and friendship. Next, because book clubs rely on great discussion topics, Chapter 3 offers six powerful "harvesting" strategies that help kids identify and capture rich questions for their clubs. These first two collections include what we might call "pre–literature circle" lessons, and in them we use short stories, articles, or poems to introduce and practice particular skills.

In Chapter 4, we move to full-scale literature circles using whole books. We begin with mini-lessons on the procedural issues of forming groups, picking books, making reading schedules, setting ground rules, and getting off to a good start. Once kids start meeting regularly, we want to steadily push them toward more substantial conversations, and to that end Chapter 5 offers six ways to nurture more thoughtful reading and conversation. Of course, difficulties will pop up in any student-led discussion group, so in Chapter 6 we've included mini-lessons covering seven of the most common group problems.

Once kids are reading and meeting reasonably well and literature circles start to hum on their own, it's a good time to highlight literary structures and elements. In Chapter 7, we offer five ways for students to more closely examine the craft of authorship. As you spark all these thoughtful conversations in your classroom, you want to keep track of what's happening. Since we want students to be self-monitoring book club members (like all lifelong readers), Chapter 8 shows five ways for students to assess their own growth as readers and talkers.

Finally, when books are completed, a well-designed culminating activity can help young readers crystallize their thinking about a book and share it with other potential readers. We're not big fans of book reports and the other lifeless projects we used to assign just to "get a grade out of literature circles." But we have found real value and literary appreciation in drama-based projects, so our last group of lessons offers five "performance projects that rock." Not only have students enjoyed these activities, both as performers and audiences, but these events have also recruited many new readers for the books being performed. Finally, in Chapter 10, we offer some tips on designing your own mini-lessons, something you'll undoubtedly want to do after reading forty-five of ours!

How Are Mini-lessons Organized in This Book?

All of our mini-lessons follow a similar but not quite identical format:

Name of the lesson

Time needed

Why do it?

Teaching the lesson

Getting started

Working the room

Reflecting

What can go wrong?

What's next?

Variations

We start each lesson with a **name**—we couldn't think of really clever ones for all forty-five, but we tried. Then we offer a **time needed** estimate, so you'll know how long the lesson should take. You may find yourself hurrying to finish inside our limits—in our own classrooms, we keep mini-lessons *really* brisk! Then we tell you **why it is worth doing,** when it might fit in, what problems the lesson can solve, or what new skills it can introduce.

Next, we take you through **teaching the lesson** step by step, beginning with detailed directions on how to **get started.** Since a literature circle meeting or other small-group discussion follows most of our mini-lessons, we've included specific tips for **working the room,** supporting and monitoring students. Then we show how you can help kids **reflect** on and debrief the experience by asking "how'd it go?" in a variety of ways. As everyone who has taught for more than five minutes is well aware, there are predictable pitfalls with almost any classroom activity, so we'll also tell you **what can go wrong** and how to avoid (or at least survive) it. For lessons that require illustration or documentation, we've included examples, which may be class handouts, charts, photographs, or samples of successful student work. If a lesson has any **variations,** offshoots, or alternative versions, we share those with you, too. And when one mini-lesson leads naturally to another, or to some great follow-up activity, we'll tell you **what's next.**

Finally, we admit to some asymmetry. We haven't provided every single section for every lesson; in some chapters, especially in Chapter 3, that would have gotten redundant. Just trust us: If a section is missing, that's because we didn't have anything to say, or what we were going to say would have bored you silly.

How Did We Choose These Forty-five Mini-lesson Topics?

Well, actually *you* (or teachers a lot like you) did. As we have traveled around the country, speaking at conferences and working in classrooms, we've been keeping a list of the questions that teachers most frequently ask. Time and again, we hear: How can I

- steer my students toward deeper comprehension?
- get kids interested in each others' ideas?
- make sure kids choose just-right books?

- help students schedule their reading and meeting time?

- deal with kids who don't do the reading?

- get kids to pay more attention to literary style and structure?

- help special education and ELL students to participate actively in book clubs?

- get kids to expand their repertoire of reading strategies?

- make sure groups are on-task when I'm not looking over their shoulder?

- introduce writing tools (including role sheets) that support student discussion?

- help shy or dominating members get the right amount of "airtime?"

- give grades for book clubs without ruining the fun?

We took these persistent questions, what we call the "Literature Circle FAQs," and built the book around them. Whether you are starting or refining literature circles in your classroom, chances are these lessons will help you address the challenges most likely to arise. And if you don't see your problem addressed, drop us an email via www.literaturecircles.com; we're still adding to that list.

How Do You Teach Mini-lessons Well?

Adapt Them to Your Class

Although you can use these mini-lessons "right out of the box," you'll need to thoughtfully customize each one. This means you'll want to

- adjust the lesson for your grade level

- personalize it for your class

- revise the timing to fit your schedule

- consider the books being read

- track your kids' reactions

Pretty soon, you'll be doing major surgery on our lessons or simply making up your own new ones. Chapter 10 gives some specific tips on do-it-yourself mini-lesson planning.

Provide Students with Journals

Literature circles involve a constantly recurring cycle of reading, writing, and talking. That means each student must have a dedicated notebook or journal for jotting notes during mini-lessons, brainstorming ideas, recording observations, setting personal goals, keeping track of skills being developed, reflecting on the day's discussion, and a dozen other uses. Literature circle journals may also be used as response logs, where students can record thoughts and questions while reading, but we will show you several other ways to accomplish this particular writing function in Chapter 3.

The format of lit circle journals doesn't matter too much. Unlined journal books are especially friendly to drawing and other nonlinguistic responses. Good old spiral notebooks are fine, too; we especially like the way the wires come unwound and lance our wrists when we collect stacks of them. The resultant bleeding highlights our teacher-as-martyr complex quite nicely!

Be Ready to Switch Roles

Teaching literature circles requires you to alternate between two quite different teacher roles: instructor and coach. When you conduct the actual mini-lessons, you will be "really teaching," as we traditionally define it. You pick the topic, provide the definition, select the materials, present the information, orchestrate the activities, monitor guided practice, and give feedback. But when students go off to their groups to apply the skills you have just taught, you switch to the role of coach or mentor. Now your job is to observe thoughtfully and provide encouragement, but mainly let the kids play the game. You are on the sidelines, seeing the fruits of your teaching from all those "practices." There may be some things you can do to affect the outcome of the day's event, but your main role now is to watch and make notes about the skills you'll need to teach or refine before the next game, and all the games after that.

Kids must understand your roles, too. They probably won't have much trouble seeing you as a "direct instructor," but the coach/mentor stance is something else. Students are not generally accustomed to classroom teachers who really let them play the game on their own. Think about what usually happens when an adult (like you) suddenly sits down in a small group of students who were assigned to work together. They shut up immediately, right? And they look at you and wait for you to tell them what to do. If there's a discussion under way, whoever is speaking now makes eye contact with you and stops looking at the other kids in the group. This phenomenon isn't surprising: We have trained students since kindergarten to look at the teacher as the boss, the source of all validation, and the one person in the room for whom you drop everything. But we cannot nurture mature, responsible literature circles—or any other substantive inquiry activities—with this mindset in place.

Therefore, you need to talk to kids explicitly about the different "yous" they will meet during the book club experience. Be especially clear about how you'll act (and how they should act) when you come around during book club meetings. You might even post a list like this:

When I sit down in your group, continue what you are doing.

You don't need to look at me or acknowledge my arrival.

I may just observe the group and move on.

If I have something to say I will say it at the appropriate moment.

Please don't ask me to give you answers or to settle debates.

As I leave, I may or may not give you a suggestion or idea to pursue.

Just think of me as a ghost.

Kids will need a few of your ghostly visits before they "get it" and become desensitized to your arrivals and departures. The biggest favor you can do for them (and for yourself) is to stick to the rules. Don't get sucked into running the groups. Don't let kids wimp out on their responsibilities, come crying to you for a bailout, and become ever more dependent. How pitiful! Sure, you're the teacher and you'll address any life-threatening problems that pop up. But mainly, use the information you gather on your visits, even the problems you notice, as fodder for the next whole-class mini-lesson.

Are These Mini-lessons Useful Only for Literature Circles?

Not at all. The three interlocking ingredients we keep harping on—effective social skills, active reading strategies, and good books—are the foundation of all kinds of engaging classroom (and life) activities. Many of our lessons build skills that people need in *any* group, large or small, literary or otherwise, in school or out. You could use many of these lessons to enhance whole-class discussions of a required book, for example. That's not exactly a book club, but it is a very common classroom structure, so why not make it work better? The same goes for almost any other collaborative classroom experience: These lessons can help kids be more thoughtful while (and after) they're watching a film, doing a science experiment, examining a primary source document, or reviewing a field trip.

When we hone students' reading strategies, we also give them tools to deal with the challenging texts they'll encounter across the rest of the curriculum. At a minimum, we can help them better understand and remember their textbook material. But that's just a start. Today, we know many teachers of science, social studies, and mathematics around the country who have started book clubs in their classrooms, using nonfiction trade books, journal articles, historical novels, research reports, primary source documents, or magazines (Daniels and Zemelman 2004). Now that's exciting! When we get kids' noses out of those 1,200-page textbooks for a few hours and put them in the kind of current, interesting nonfiction that thoughtful adults are reading, then we are really inviting them into lifelong literacy.

Does Scientific Research Support Literature Circles?

You bet. In these days when the call for "scientific proof" is loud and clear, it is important to show that recommended classroom practices really work.

Teachers need to know that their "gut instincts" are backed by a large body of supportive research. Scores of confirming studies, using both quantitative and qualitative methodologies of rigorous design, validate the worth of book clubs. Book club–type discussions have been linked to higher reading achievement at a variety of grade levels and among students who are poor, inner-city, bilingual, ESL, or incarcerated (Daniels 2001). The National Assessment of Educational Progress (NAEP, our nation's standardized-test report card) shows that kids who do large amounts of independent reading score about 10 percent higher on reading tests than kids who read little or not at all. And 10 percent is a huge difference—on the NAEP test, a 1 percent difference can be statistically significant—and the difference between low scores and high ones is relatively narrow.

Harvey's book *Literature Circles: Voice and Choice in Book Clubs and Reading Groups* (2001) offers a sampling of the more current studies. A summary may also be found on www.literaturecircles.com. With our colleague Steve Zemelman, Harvey has written two summaries of broader reading research issues, along with some commentary on the difficulty of getting such research into the hands of classroom teachers (Daniels, Zemelman, and Bizar 1999; Zemelman, Daniels, and Bizar 1999).

Undoubtedly the most comprehensive bibliography on literature circle research and practice has been compiled by Ian Wilkinson, P. Karen Murphy, and Anna O. Soter as part of a federally funded effort to identify promising practices in literacy education (Sweet 2003). As this book goes to press, these researchers are in the middle of a three-year study entitled "Group Discussions as Mechanism for Promoting High-Level Comprehension of Text." All teachers using literature circles will surely look forward to their findings.

What About Educational Standards?

The emerging research on book clubs is just one spur to their popularity. The fact that kids and teachers simply love literature circle time is certainly another driving factor. But the book club boom has also been sparked by the national curriculum standards in English language arts, developed by the National Council of Teachers of English and International Reading Association (1996), which have been officially adopted by many states and districts. Among other outcomes, these national standards require that:

- Students read a wide range of print and nonprint texts to build an understanding of texts, of themselves, and of the cultures of the United States and the world; to acquire new information; to respond to the needs and demands of society and the workplace; and for personal fulfillment. These texts include both fiction and nonfiction, classic and contemporary works.

- Students read a wide range of literature from many periods in many genres to build an understanding of the many dimensions (philosophical, ethical, aesthetic) of human experience.

The NCTE and IRA don't stop with general support for rich and wide-ranging reading experiences. Their standards go on to specifically endorse book clubs as a "best practice" and recommend them for America's young readers (Sierra-Perry 1996).

Actually, the standards documents discuss literature circles under the heading "Book Clubs: Reading Just for Fun." Now, that's a pretty bold label to use in times when public talk about education favors terms such as "get tough," "add rigor," "buckle down," "be accountable," or "line up for the next test." But the NCTE/IRA framers know literacy, they know kids, and they know how lifelong readers are raised. Schooling that's filled with solitary and mechanical work, frustration, and failure doesn't bond kids to reading. People who read and think and grow for a lifetime typically fell in love with books at an early age, and often, a teacher was the matchmaker.

Who Are We?

Since we will be spending the next two hundred pages with you, we thought it might be helpful to introduce ourselves. The two of us have been working with literature circles—and with each other—for quite a while. Nancy is in her twenty-seventh year of teaching at Victor J. Andrew High School in Tinley Park, Illinois, where her classes include basic and honors Language Arts and American Studies. As a top-level graduate of Johnson and Johnson collaborative learning training, it has been natural for Nancy to apply the insights of cooperative learning to reading structures like literature circles. Nancy's book *Reading and Writing Together: Collaborative Literacy in Action* (2002) shows how a teacher committed to a highly interdependent classroom operates, from September through June. Each summer, Nancy and Harvey teach together at the Walloon Institute, which brings staff development on reading and writing across the curriculum to teachers around the country.

Harvey began teaching in Chicago in 1969 and later taught English and social studies at Lake Forest High School, still one of American's finest places for young people. Since the initial publication of his *Literature Circles: Voice and Choice in Book Clubs and Reading Groups* in 1994, "Smokey" has been able to work with teachers and students across the country, borrowing the best ideas from the brightest teachers and refining and improving the book club model. This "second wave" of structures and strategies fed a new edition of the book, published in 2001. He has also written several other books on literacy and school reform with various combinations of colleagues Steven Zemelman, Marilyn Bizar, and Art Hyde. Among these are *Subjects Matter: Every Teacher's Guide to Content-Area Reading; Methods That Matter; Best Practice: New Standards for Teaching and Learning in America's Schools;* and *Rethinking High School.*

Why do we mention all these other books? We're not just trying to establish our bona fides here, although readers have a right to know where their authors come from. And all our books do make lovely gifts. But the main point is: We have written a lot of other stuff about book clubs and collaborative strategies that we will not be repeating here. This book focuses narrowly (and purposely) on just one part of the book club picture. Yes, mini-lessons are a really big part of book clubs—but still, they're not the whole story.

If you want to learn more about starting book clubs, training students, building a classroom library, developing assessments, or other day-to-day matters, please take a look at our other materials. Come to think of it, we are not the only people with good things to say about literature circles. There are a number of teacher-author colleagues, from Washington State to Maine, who've written really helpful books about literature circles for young readers. So, we'll close this chapter with a recommended reading list—sources where you might find answers to questions we don't address here or even, God forbid, hear the views of people who don't always do it our way.

Welcome to our book! We hope it works for you and your students. If you have responses or stories to share, or just need a literary shoulder to cry on, you can reach us through our website, www.literaturecircles.com.

Why the Starfish?

The starfish motif throughout this book comes from a fortuitous vacation snapshot Harvey took last winter. While walking a deserted stretch of Caribbean beach, "Smokey" and his wife came upon a tiny inlet where a half-dozen big red starfish were lying in about a foot of water. Probably because both of us are unnaturally preoccupied with teaching, the array of five-legged starfish reminded us of a classroom with several student-led book clubs meeting at once. We've always thought that five members is the ideal size for literature circle discussions. With this number of students, groups are big enough to include many different points of view, but small enough to provide positive social pressure for every kid to join in. There is no bigger "boss leg"; all five members bear equal responsibility for the functioning of the whole organism. And when all members contribute energetically, the group takes on a beautiful life of its own. (But four works very well too, and starfish are much quieter than kids in book clubs!)

When Nancy saw the starfish photo, she came up with the most far-fetched but maybe most important analogy of all: When you cut off a starfish's leg, it will regenerate to become whole (at least in some species). We hope that even when classroom literature circles disband, our students will continue to be enthusiastic readers, talking about books with their friends and growing the network of readers throughout our country.

Recommended Readings

Daniels, Harvey. 2001. *Literature Circles: Voice and Choice in Book Clubs and Reading Groups, Second Edition.* Portland, ME: Stenhouse.

Daniels, Harvey, and Marilyn Bizar. 1998. *Methods That Matter: Six Structures for Best Practice Classrooms.* Portland, ME: Stenhouse.

Hill, Bonnie Campbell, Katherine Schlick-Noe, and Janine King. 2003. *Literature Circles in Middle School.* Norwood, MA: Christopher-Gordon.

Hill, Bonnie Campbell, Nancy Johnson, and Katherine Schlick-Noe. 2000. *Literature Circles Resource Guide.* Norwood, MA: Christopher-Gordon.

Hill, Bonnie Campbell, Nancy Johnson, and Katherine Schlick-Noe. 1995. *Literature Circles and Response.* Norwood, MA: Christopher-Gordon.

McMahon, Susan, Taffy Raphael, Virginia Goatley, and Laura Pardo. 1997. *The Book Club Connection.* New York: Teachers College Press.

Raphael, Taffy, Laura Pardo, and Kathy Highfield. 2002. *Book Club: A Literature-Based Curriculum*. Lawrence, MA: Small Planet Communications.

Samway, Katherine Davies, and Gail Whang. 1996. *Literature Study Circles in a Multicultural Classroom*. Portland, ME: Stenhouse.

Schlick-Noe, Katherine, and Barbara Johnson. 1999. *Getting Started with Literature Circles*. Norwood, MA: Christopher-Gordon.

Steineke, Nancy. 2002. *Reading and Writing Together: Collaborative Literacy in Action*. Portsmouth, NH: Heinemann.

c h a p t e r

2

Getting Ready for Peer-Led Discussions

Putting kids into literature circles is a lot like being able to trust them in a fancy restaurant. If you took your students on a fine-dining excursion, they'd need to have table manners, negotiate the menu, know which utensils to use and when, stay seated, make pleasant conversation without disturbing other diners, and deal with unexpected circumstances graciously, such as when the soup does not come in a bowl but in the shell of a sea urchin. Our guess is that right now, with no preparation, you might not be confident taking your class on that restaurant field trip, even if their pricey meals were covered by a special arts grant. However, if such an outing really were your goal, we fully believe that you could teach your students the basic skills necessary for a pleasant and civilized meal.

The same is true for literature circles. If book clubs are your goal, then it's important first to create a community in which they can thrive by establishing the following foundation:

- Students know the other members of the class as individuals.

- Students treat each other well, listen to each other, and avoid put-downs.

- Students understand and practice key social skills when interacting with others.

- Students understand and practice specific thinking skills when reading text.

The good news is that it's probably a lot easier to prepare kids for literature circles than for that big night on the town!

Depending on your students' backgrounds, you might need to spend a lot of time on these skills or just a little. If kids know the reading strategies and have done lots of collaborative learning, you can zoom ahead and skip some of the initial mini-lessons. But if in doubt, slow down, and take the time to do some of these pre–lit circle lessons. Even veteran groups will enjoy these activities; they build deeper acquaintances and interdependence among the kids and reinforce the ways smart readers think.

Class Icebreaker: Find Someone Who

Why Do It?

It is human nature to share ideas more easily and fully with people we know. At the same time, left to their own devices, students will automatically gravitate toward their friends when given a choice of small-group assignments. Quick icebreakers offer a good way for students to expand their working relationships beyond their immediate friends. When class members already have some acquaintance with people outside their fifth-hour clique, they will be far less likely to throw tantrums when their book clubs include kids they do not know well. Also, initiating a conversation with someone new, the social skill honed in icebreaking, is useful in almost any employment situation. Find Someone Who gives students a low-risk opportunity to briefly interview classmates they might not normally talk to. It's a good activity to use in the beginning of the year and then resurrect about a week before book clubs will be formed.

Teaching the Lesson

Getting Started

Students begin with a list of topics written on a grid (see the blank Find Someone Who sheet in the appendix). Demonstrate the following steps with one student as the class carefully watches. (Check out the completed Find Someone Who exercise on page 33.)

1. Find Someone Who requires you to get up out of your chairs and mingle. Since you'll also be taking some notes, be sure to carry your journal or binder with you so that you'll have a hard surface to write on.

2. Wave your paper above your head to signal that you need a partner. Find a category that applies to your new partner, conduct a brief interview on the topic, and write the information in the box.

3. Have your partner sign under the information. This is the *only* time your partner will write on your paper.

4. Print your partner's first and last name underneath his or her signature.

5. Find a new partner and fill in a different topic.

6. You must have a different partner for each topic box.

7. Once you've filled in the designated number of boxes, you may sit down. However, those who are still looking for partners may interview those who are seated.

Working the Room

As students mingle, you should roam the room, nudging wallflowers out of the corner and helping shyer students connect with partners by pointing out those who are free. Students will also try to bunch up with a group of friends. These clusters are very effective in shutting out remaining class members, so remind the kids that pairing off means they are with only one other person, and there is significant space between pairs!

Reflecting

Some students may have done this exercise before in another class, and assume that it is just another "time waster" activity. Therefore, after students have completed their sheets, it's important that they also analyze the process. Ask this question: What specific social skills were you using as you completed this assignment? Have students brainstorm with a partner or on their own and then compile a master list. Students will be amazed at how much they were doing when all of the ideas are combined.

A Completed "Find Someone Who" Sheet

FIND SOMEONE WHO...

NAME Amal

DATE 1/23/04   HOUR 5

VISITED ANOTHER COUNTRY	HAS A FAVORITE SPECTATOR SPORT
Mexico Nikki Nicole	Football Ron Ron
HAS FAVORITE PIZZA TOPPINGS	**HAS A FAVORITE JUNK FOOD**
Pepperoni Bridget Bridget	Doritos Jason
RENTED A MOVIE	**WENT TO SEE A MOVIE**
Uptown girls Brittany Brittany	Something's got to go walter Walter
SEEN A STAGE PLAY	**HAS A FAVORITE BOOK**
Once on an island Lisa Lisa	Perks of being a wallflower Mal Mal
SHOPS AT FAVORITE STORE	**HAS A FAVORITE RESTAURANT**
Champs: It's in mall Anthony Anthony	Red Lobster Brittany Brittany
LIKES WINTER WEATHER—WHY?	**DRIVES A CAR—MAKE/MODEL**
Fun to play in snow Roy harm	Camero Rick Rick
HATES A VEGETABLE	**LOVES A VEGETABLE**
Spinach Ryan	Corn Bob Bob
HAS SIBLINGS: #, AGE, GENDER	**IS AN ONLY CHILD— ADVANTAGES/DISADVANTAGES**
1 sister 12	parents spend all time on you; no one to blame stuff on mrs. Stieneke

A blank version of this form can be found in the appendix.

"Find Someone Who" Skills

Using Eye Contact
being polite
smiling
concentrating on partner
following directions
using quiet voices
being friendly
being nice - not criticizing answers
leaving differences outside classroom
shaking hands
being quiet when waving paper
showing respect
introducing yourself
managing time
not being shy
giving detailed answers
taking notes
meeting new people
being patient
being helpful
laughing - having fun
listening

After students copy this master list on the back of their Find Someone Who sheets, have them reflect on their own performance and list three things they could do better the next time the class uses this icebreaker.

What Can Go Wrong?

First, it works much better to do half the chart one day and then finish it the following day. If you observe kids at work for a while, you can pinpoint problems that can then be discussed before the activity is completed. A common problem is that boys talk only to boys and girls talk only to girls. When we notice this occurring, we say, "It looks like a lot of you are talking only to those of the same gender. To get full credit on this activity, you need to interview at least seven members of the opposite sex."

As you monitor, you'll find that some students will try to park themselves in one spot and wait for others to approach them. It's important to get them to move around because the only people who will come to them will be their friends.

Watch out for students shoving sheets at each other while saying, "Write down what kind of pizza you like and sign your name." If students are having their partners do all the writing, they can easily complete the entire sheet without actually meeting and conversing with anyone.

Finally, remember that Find Someone Who requires that all students be out of their seats, so be sure to assess their maturity level before letting them loose!

Variations

It's very important to use this activity more than once because students will be much better at it the second time. On the second Find Someone Who, students can work on the three improvement goals they set the first time. Also, between the first and second exercises, have students brainstorm new topic ideas—they can use these for the second go-round. For a more personalized twist, ask students to submit a piece of information (school-appropriate, of course) that they think no one else knows about them. Using that info, you can easily create a new and personalized Find Someone Who handout for each class. The Find Someone Who—Brainstormed New Topic List shows some of the personal experiences and interests one class came up with. This time the searching will be a bit more challenging since some of the topics fit only one or two classmates. Of course, even if the questioner knows someone who, for instance, likes reggae, she still needs to interview them about their favorite reggae bands and songs.

Find Someone Who—Brainstormed New Topic List

1. Snowboards
2. Plays chess
3. Speaks another language
4. Broke a bone
5. Has a birthday in January
6. Loves to ice skate
7. Likes reggae
8. Had chickenpox
9. Travels to compete internationally
10. Ate 40 Chicken McNuggets in under 6 minutes
11. High jumps for the track team
12. Has been to Mexico
13. Can fix a flat tire
14. Works at a bowling alley
15. Can tell you a lot about WWII
16. Can play heavy/maniac mode on *Dance Dance Revolution*
17. Skateboards
18. Plays badminton
19. Has a dog
20. Has a chicken
21. Has six siblings
22. Plays the drums

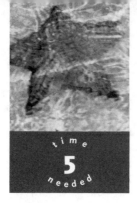

time
5
needed

Conversational Warm-up: Membership Grid

Why Do It?

We've noticed that students tend to stick with their friends rather than take the risk of getting to know someone new. When a literature circle is formed around a chosen book rather than preexisting friendships, discussion may stall if students can't "break the ice." Giving groups a low-risk, nonacademic topic to discuss every time they meet, just before they start the official book work, helps students to develop friendly working relationships. The Membership Grid is a fun way for students to get to know each other using a quick interview format.

Teaching the Lesson

Getting Started

Students begin with a blank Membership Grid (you can find one in the appendix). The date and interview topics are recorded on the left and the group members' names on the right above the columns. The less students know about each other, the more frequently groups should do this activity. In the beginning of the year, it's not a bad idea for students to discuss a grid topic every day, even though they might be having official book club meetings just once or twice a week. Groups discuss a different topic each time they use the grid. This could be a topic you assign or a topic the group negotiates on its

Student-Suggested Grid Topics

Places you've traveled
Plans after high school
Worst/favorite school subject
What type of music do you listen to?
Things you do on the weekend
Favorite amusement park rides
Favorite restaurant
Favorite fast food
Favorite car
Favorite cookies
Favorite movie
Favorite store at the mall
Favorite TV show
What did you do the day before?
Most embarrassing moment
Plans for spring break
Preference: carpet vs. wood
Preference: Coke vs. Pepsi
Favorite pizza
What sports do you play?
What sports do you watch?
Hobbies?
If you were stuck on a deserted island, what would you bring?
Favorite action hero
Best presents you've received/given
Celebrity you'd like to date
Part-time jobs
Favorite book
What do you look for when it comes to the opposite sex?
Favorite place to get ice cream

own. When groups choose their own topics, remind them that they must remain "school-appropriate." (Student-Suggested Grid Topics shows some typical choices.)

The group then takes about one minute to interview each member in turn. As the group conducts each interview, the members take notes on each person's answers. The goal is to ask the interviewee enough questions about the topic to elicit some interesting details, which members then write on their grid. In the column under their own name, students may either jot notes on what they said when they were interviewed or write some of the questions they asked when they interviewed the others. Of course, the covert goal of the Membership Grid is to have groups practice the same focusing and questioning that is necessary for an in-depth discussion about a book. Even later in the year, after students are better acquainted, it is still important

Filled-in Membership Grid

MEMBERSHIP GRID   Stephanie

TOPICS	GROUP MEMBERS			
	Kim	Krystle	Amanda	Mike
9-24 all time fav. movie	Pearl Harbor -Josh Hartnett - when he dies -12 times	Grease -Jon Travolta -owns it -2 times a day -Carnival	Walk to Remember -cute, romance -no, doesn't own	Star Ship Troopers -bloody scenes -Frank -owns movie
10-3 Halloween	be Kim -no trick or treating -candy -box of popcorn	-Alan -no trick or treating -little mermaid bride -haunted house	-be Amanda -Bunny rabbit -haunted house -snickers	-ninja -fav. costume was ninja -trick or treating -heath bars
10-10 weekend	Lincoln Way's homecoming - with boyfriend -friends house after dance	I.S.U. -going w/friends -Lindseys sister -college visit	Great America -friends from Plainfield -friends driving -Raging Bull	rest -in bed -visit his dad in Romeoville
10-15 Cubbies!	Sox fan -no fav player -watched 42 secs. game	Cubs fan -Sammy Sosa -watched game -yes, win series	Sox fan -watched game -should of won -should have gotten beaten.	Sox fan -turned off game -not going to win series -Alou-favorite player

A blank version of this form can be found in the appendix.

to begin book club meetings with the Membership Grid. It is a great warm-up that helps ensure better academic discussion.

Working the Room

The most important thing to emphasize is not to interview classmates too quickly. Interviewers should use the full minute for each member before moving on. However, as students get to know each other better and start to enjoy the Membership Grid conversations, your monitoring goal may change. You may soon have to push students through their interviews because they will be perfectly willing to continue their ice-breaking conversations well beyond the allotted five minutes!

Reflecting

The best time to debrief is after two or three interviews. Students should review their note-taking and interview skills so they can set some improvement goals. While better questions create livelier interviews, students also find that taking more-detailed notes creates better reading later; they often find that it is fun to look back on these grids and recall specific conversations.

What Can Go Wrong?

Sometimes groups won't be very good at interviewing. Watch to see if any groups are asking too many yes/no questions. You may have to give those groups a little private coaching. If you assign a topic to the class and a group complains about it, just tell the students to think of a different "school-appropriate" topic.

The biggest problem you might face arises if you ask some members to share their grid answers with the whole class. It's almost guaranteed that the kid you call on will say something bizarre. For example, in Nancy's American Literature class one day, the juniors were having some serious discussions concerning their post-graduation plans. However, in the large-group forum, one student confidently volunteered that he was going to be a drug dealer. Okay, thank you for sharing; let's turn to our lit circle novels. Later, when Nancy looked at this kid's grid, it revealed that he had talked at length about going to the University of Illinois to study engineering. When asked why he said drug dealer instead of engineer, the young man replied, "Drug dealer seemed like a funnier answer." The moral of the story is that students often do better personal sharing in a small group than with the whole class.

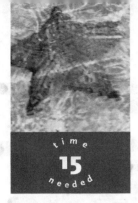

Home Court Advantage

Why Do It?

The use of the put-down for humorous effect can probably be traced back to the pilot episode of *I Love Lucy*, and *Friends* definitely continued the tradition. Though the sitcoms make us laugh, the problem with real-life put-downs is that they quickly create an atmosphere of mistrust. If classmates cannot trust one another, they are highly unlikely to share opinions or even listen to each other. Furthermore, recent brain imaging research demonstrates that the social wounds caused by rejection create a reaction very similar to physical pain (*Chicago Tribune* 2003). Consequently, it's almost impossible to do any higher-order thinking when negative emotions have taken center stage. Students need to understand the damage put-downs can do and learn how to avoid them. Home Court Advantage helps students to think about why teams win more home games than away games and then use those insights to create a "winning" classroom.

Teaching the Lesson

Getting Started

The best way to start is with the sports pages of your local paper. Announce the standings of your home teams and point out the difference in wins between home and away games. As you compare some sports, the class will notice that teams typically win more games at home. This pattern is statistically proven and is consistent whether the teams are professional or amateur. This leads to the question: *Why do teams win more games at home than away?* Give students a couple of minutes to work with a partner and list as many reasons as possible.

Now have the pairs review their lists and rank their reasons in order of importance, with number one being the most important. Then work with the class to compile a master list, getting a suggestion from each pair. Tell students to give their highest-ranking item that hasn't already been mentioned; if all of their reasons have been taken, they should repeat the item they ranked number one. The master list will look something like the Home Court List shown here.

After creating the list, conclude by telling the class that one of the most important ways to keep the home court advantage is to avoid using put-downs. From now on, if anyone hears a put-down, just gently say "home

Home Court List—Fifth Hour, 1/13/04

More fans
No distracting fans
People you know are there
Practiced on the same court
Defending your home town
Motivated - play harder to please
    the fans
The whole team is there
Feel more relaxed
More confidence

court" to remind that person to stop. Don't accept the kids' excuses that they are "only joking." When a joke is at the expense of another person, it's not a joke, it's a put-down.

Working the Room

The most challenging aspect of this activity is getting kids to remember to maintain their home court advantage. This mini-lesson is often taught in the first week or two of school, so the trick is to get the kids to keep using it in November. A poster you can point to is helpful. Also, if you hear a put-down and no one responds, jump in with a "home court!" of your own.

Reflecting

From time to time, it's good to have kids return to the home court idea by writing in their journals. Here are some prompts that work:

> How have you helped to make this class a winning home court experience?

> What have you personally done to make sure the home court rule is followed?

> How have you contributed to the learning and positive support of your fellow team members?

Rather than asking kids to share these writings aloud, we let them stand as personal assessments. The writing itself encourages thinking and taking responsibility. Also, as the year progresses, students do realize that it is much easier to take risks when they are not constantly afraid of what others might blurt out in the name of humor.

What Can Go Wrong?

Once in a while, students come up with an odd reason for Home Court Advantage. We'll never forget the pair of boys who gave wives/girlfriends as an advantage. When asked how this helped the team, the boys explained with straight faces that since the players would be able to have sex the night before the game, they would be calmer, better rested, and more relaxed as they played. Possibly so, but that wasn't something we were going to put on a big chart for the principal to see. We got the guys to agree to "greater family/ friend support." Sometimes students really mean something legitimate but don't phrase it well. Other times an idea just won't fly in the school environment, and they need to submit something more suitable.

Variations

If you have a little time to spare, have the kids work with partners to make "Home Court" posters. We give these instructions:

> *You need to create a poster that says Home Court in big letters. Along with that you need a graphic and a slogan that will remind people that we're all on the same team as well as being fans of one another. If you still have room, add other encouraging words and phrases that will remind classmates to keep our Home Court Advantage alive.*

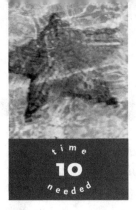

Defining Discussion Skills

Why Do It?

As students begin to engage in small-group discussions, we can guarantee that their skills won't be perfect. Groups often reflect a continuum: A couple of groups will click, a few more will operate superficially, and one or two will spend their time arguing or ignoring each other. The trick is to observe these interactions carefully and make a list of specific skills that groups appear to be lacking. Then have the groups make their own lists by asking this question: "When a group has a really good discussion about what they've read, what kinds of things are the members saying and doing?" Once groups have their lists, we tell them to draw lines through the behaviors they know they're doing consistently. What's left are the things they need to work on.

Now that the students have recognized what they could do better, the next step is to get them to change their interaction patterns. The best way to begin this process is by defining a specific discussion skill with a T-chart. Though any social skill can be defined in this way, we like to start groups off with a discussion of friendliness and support since the most effective work groups are those in which the members actively show their support and appreciation of one another. Also, when members treat each other well, people feel more invested in each other and are more likely to come better prepared for discussion.

Teaching the Lesson

Getting Started

Have students open to a clean page in their journals and ____ and Support at the top edge, then fold the page in half len____ two columns. They then label the left-hand column "Look____ right-hand column "Sounds Like." Be sure to create your own____ with the class. An overhead transparency works best because at____ you have a copy of the T-chart the class created. Then we say:

> *Treating people with friendliness and support is essential for getting along and creating enjoyable working relationships. The T-chart is a way to show some specific examples of how you can start using this skill more in your groups. When you look at the T-chart, the left-hand column defines what someone would look like using the skill, what kind of body language an observer would see. The right-hand column lists actual phrases people could say; think in terms of a script, sentences and phrases that would go in quotes.*

Next we give students one or two examples to write down in each column. "Looks Like" might include "giving eye contact" and "sitting close together." "Sounds Like" might include "Hi, what's up?" and "That's a good idea; I didn't think of that." As you give the examples, emphasize that "Looks Like" refers to body language, while "Sounds Like" should be phrases people would actually say; they should go in quotes. All examples should of course demonstrate positive behaviors.

We're careful to stress that the item in one column does not need to directly correspond with the idea across from it in the other column. Each column is just a list of examples. All examples, whether they are "Looks Like" or "Sounds Like," focus on the same skill, but each column stands on its own.

After giving your suggestions, have students work in pairs to brainstorm additional items for both columns. Remind students to keep the lists positive; they should be listing behaviors to cultivate, not ones to avoid. Here's what we say: "Okay, here's an example of what *not* to write down on a T-chart:

shut up so that someone else can talk!' If you say that to someone, a good chance the discussion won't improve. First of all, what's the al problem here?" The kids will quickly recognize that one person is monopolizing the conversation. "Since that's the problem, what's something positive members could say that would solve it?" Positive examples might include, "Let's let someone different go first this time" or "That was a very thorough answer; who has a different idea?"

If this is the first time students have worked with a T-chart, the task will seem foreign and strange; don't be surprised if they have a hard time coming up with a lot of examples. However, if each pair comes up with two or three ideas for each side, you will still end up with a substantial list for each column by the time you combine everyone's suggestions.

Two or three minutes are plenty of time for the brainstorming. Call time and then just go around the room, having each pair contribute a "Looks Like" or "Sounds Like" for the classroom chart. If any of the examples are negative, help the pair rephrase the idea in a more positive way. As you copy the T-chart ideas on the overhead, students should be writing them in their journals.

The best way to immediately reinforce the use of a new T-chart skill is to have students use it in a short discussion; most skills can be practiced during

Friendliness and Support T-Chart

Friendliness and Support	
Looks Like	Sounds Like
Giving eye contact	"Hi, what's up?"
Sitting close together	"That was a good idea. I didn't think of that."
Smiling	"Hi, how are you today?"
Nodding in agreement	"What do you think?"
Desks touching	"Thank you."
Eye contact	"Let's hear from everybody before we decide."
People taking turns speaking	"That's interesting; tell us more about your idea."
Taking notes on what others say	"Wow, I didn't think of that."

a Membership Grid conversation. Another quick way to practice is to have the students read a very short story or poem, jotting down questions or underlining some passages to discuss. Then students move into their groups and lead a short discussion with the goal of using the selected T-chart skill as much as possible. The use of a short text to hone skills and experiment with discussion techniques is outlined in the next chapter, Practicing with Short Text.

Working the Room

As students engage in discussion, require that they have their journals open to the whole-class T-chart created earlier. Tell them that you're observing their groups for the friendliness and support skills listed, and you want them to use the chart as much as possible. When groups remember, give them the thumbs up. If they've forgotten the skill, you might interrupt the group and say, "I haven't heard anybody say anything from the T-chart. Let's hear something from each person now."

Reflecting

When students begin practicing a new skill, have them jot notes in their journal about how they felt using it. While they're writing, walk around and read over their shoulders so that you can note the helpful responses (versus some variation of the "This sucked!" diatribe) and call on those kids a little later. Typically students will write that they felt stupid, uncomfortable, unnatural, and so forth. That's exactly how they should feel. A new discussion skill that is not already a natural part of a person's behavior is going to feel that way. Gaining further expertise requires going through four stages:

1. Awkwardness—Because the new T-chart language is so uncomfortable, students will try to avoid using it and will probably tell you that it is a stupid idea. Ignore them.

2. Phoniness—Students give up trying to talk you out of the T-chart and are resigned to practicing the behaviors. It sounds fake and sing-songy. That's okay.

Sample T-Charts

Encouraging Participation

Looks Like	Sounds Like
Eye Contact	Using names
Desks close together	"What do you think?"
Leaning in	"Let's hear from (name)"
Focus on the speaker	"Give us an idea (name)"
Looking interested	"Let (name) go first this time"

Clearing up Confusing Parts of the Story

Looks Like	Sounds Like
Eye Contact	"where did that part start?"
Books open to same page	"Let's sum up what we've just said."
Leaning in	"which characters were in that scene?"
Focus on the speaker	"what was going on here, I couldn't follow it?"
Looking Interested	"what does this part have to do with what happened earlier?"
Taking Notes	"How did you figure that out? What were the clues?"

3. Overuse—Next you may notice students competing with each other to see how many times they can use the skill. As a matter a fact, you might wonder whether the skill is getting in the way of any substantial academic conversation. When you see students in this stage, congratulate yourself. They are beginning to own the skill and soon they'll be using it appropriately.

4. Integration—Students use the skill when it needs to be used and also recognize the positive effect the skill has on the group's work. At this point you might hear students complaining about the lousy groups they're in elsewhere during the day. Now that they understand what it takes to be a good member, it's hard for them to understand why the students in their other classes haven't figured this out!

When you discuss the skill reflection as a whole class, be sure to call on some kids who wrote about their discomfort. Then explain the four stages of expertise to them. If they had been totally at ease with the friendliness and support activity, it would mean that they had developed finesse and it was time to work on some other skill! Also, be sure to point out that even though using the T-chart language made them feel uncomfortable, you noticed that the groups were smiling and more animated and engaged in their discussions.

What Can Go Wrong?

As we mentioned earlier, the more uncomfortable students are with a new social skill, the more they will actively fight you on it. They will not hesitate to tell you, "This sucks . . . this is stupid . . . this is a waste of time . . . you're the teacher; why aren't you teaching us?" All of these comments have one goal: to make you give up and let the complainers fall back into their old, comfortable ways. Ironically, any student who manifests such resistance has little concept of support and friendliness and therefore needs your coaching more than they know! Showing support and friendliness is the absolute cornerstone skill for creating a class where literature circles will excel. No high-level academic discussion will ever take place unless students are nice to each other. You are older, wiser, and more determined than your students. You can persevere longer than they can resist!

Skills That Can Be Defined with T-Charts

- Asking follow-up questions so that people explain their answers in more detail
- Being friendly
- Staying focused on the group
- Listening to everyone's ideas
- Keeping everyone in the group involved
- Recognizing members' good ideas
- Welcoming diverse viewpoints
- Disagreeing constructively, with confidence and enthusiasm
- Extending discussion on a topic
- Paraphrasing
- Attentive listening
- Building on one another's ideas (piggybacking)
- Directing the group's work
- Using the text to support an idea
- Asking clarification questions when confused

Variations

After encouraging students to use the Friendliness and Support T-Chart in a couple of discussions, have them return to the "Sounds Like" column and brainstorm new phrases. You'll find that this time students will be more creative and prolific in their brainstorming. Also, remember that the T-chart is the best way to introduce and define other discussion skills that students need to hone. Take a look at Skills That Can Be Defined with T-Charts.

time
30
needed

(three 10-minute sessions)

Think-Aloud

Why Do It?

Believe it or not, a lot of kids have never realized that reading and thinking are interrelated. For many, reading means scanning the page from left to right and top to bottom, but doesn't include an ongoing mental conversation or even remembering what one has read. The thinking skills that good readers take for granted are the same skills that poor readers are unaware of. Therefore, it's important for the teacher to model these thinking skills so that students can see the connection between reading and thinking (Farr 2004). Kids must actively

- monitor,
- identify,
- practice, and
- revise

their reading/thinking strategies. (See Chapter 1, Reading Strategies.)

Teaching the Lesson

Getting Started

We introduce the connection between reading and thinking by saying, "Think about a time when you experienced a 'reader space-out,' a time when you read something but didn't remember a thing about it afterwards. Why do you think this happened?" Likely responses include

"I didn't understand it."

"I was thinking about something else."

"I never remember what I read."

We segue by saying, "Reading and thinking go hand in hand. If you work to actually think about what you're reading while you read, you'll remember a lot more. That's why I'm going to read something aloud and show you what I'm thinking while I'm reading."

Choose a short piece of text (a nonfiction article, short story, poem, or novel excerpt). Before making photocopies for the class, mark three or four dots on the text to indicate where you will stop and think aloud about the text. After passing out the text piece, tell students that you will stop at the dots and briefly tell them what you were thinking at those points. As you stop and explain, the students should listen carefully and jot down some notes on the text so that they can go back later and remember what you said.

Read the text aloud, stopping at the predetermined dots. As you think aloud, make it lively but brief. Real thinking while reading is a continual and rapid internal conversation, not a series of speeches! Remind students to listen and jot down some notes. Here's an example using the poem "Ozymandias" by Percy Bysshe Shelley.

Text	Think-Aloud
I met a traveler from an antique land Who said: "Two vast and trunkless legs of stone Stand in the desert. Near them, on the sand ●	*The sand and the word antique makes me think of Egypt; the sphinx is thousands of years old. It's weird how the legs are still standing. (prior knowledge-connection, judgment)*
Half sunk, a shattered visage lies, whose frown And wrinkled lip, and sneer of cold command, ●	*I picture the rest of the statue mostly buried with just the*

Text	Think-Aloud

face sticking out. It makes me think of those statues on Easter Island; they're frowning too. (visualization, prior knowledge-connection)

Tell that its sculptor well those passions read
Which yet survive, stamped on these lifeless
   things,
The hand that mockt them and the heart
   that fed; ●

I wonder if this means the sculptor purposely made the guy who posed for the statue look bad? I'm not sure whose heart the poet means. (inference, wondering/question)

And on the pedestal these words appear
'My name is Ozymandias, king of kings.
Look on my works, ye Mighty, and despair!' ●

Wow, Ozymandias thought he was really something, very powerful. When he says, "Look on my works, ye Mighty," it sounds like he's challenging God. (judgment, inference)

Nothing beside remains. Round the decay
Of that colossal wreck, boundless and bare ●

Looks like old Oz wasn't so powerful after all. His statue has fallen apart and once that quote gets chipped off, no one will even know who the statue was supposed to be. (drawing a conclusion, opinion)

Text	Think-Aloud
The lone and level sands stretch far away." ●	*This line reminds me of the end of Planet of the Apes when Charlton Heston is riding along the beach and finds the Statue of Liberty buried up to its neck in sand. I wonder how people hundreds of years from now will interpret our landmarks. (prior knowledge-connection, question)*

After the reading, have students compare notes with a partner, jotting down think-aloud details that you mentioned but they failed to write down. Next, again with their partners, students should look over the teacher comments and try to label them according to the thinking skills that were used. In other words, they are to describe what kind of thinking was going on.

Finally, examine the think-aloud dots as a whole class. This "game show" introduction makes it fun: "And now we will be playing a few rounds of 'What was the teacher thinking?'" Then call on a few students at random for each of the dots. The first student describes what the teacher was thinking while the second student describes the type of thinking. Be sure to write down the thinking labels in the students' own words rather than translating them into teacher-speak. Keep a running list of reading/thinking skills on the overhead and have students copy them in their journals.

Try to model a few Think-Alouds over a three-day period whenever you are introducing a new genre. (We give the lesson time as thirty minutes, but that really means ten minutes per day for three days.) For the second Think-Aloud, students consult their reading/thinking skills lists from the previous day. Follow the same procedure as outlined earlier, but during the large-group discussion, refer back to the list, checking off the skills that were used as well as adding new skills.

Student Think-Aloud Example—Hazing

Students Face Discipline in Hazing Case

By Lisa Black
Tribune staff reporter
May 6, 2003

Having watched videotapes of what one school administrator called the "deplorable" hazing of young women during a touch football game that escalated into punching, shoving and mud-lobbing, Glenbrook North High School officials today said they are considering disciplinary action against some students.

Though the incident happened off campus, students who are members of extracurricular activities and athletics could be disciplined for violating the Code of Conduct they signed at the beginning of the school year, said Diane Freeman, spokeswoman for Northfield Township High School District 225, which includes Glenbrook North.

Police also are viewing the tapes and are considering criminal charges in the incident, which sent five girls with minor injuries to a local hospital. One participant sustained a broken ankle, and another had to receive stitches to her head, authorities said. ●

The fracas erupted at a powder-puff football game, played secretly in the Chipilly Woods Forest Preserve about 11 A.M. Sunday, authorities said. About 100 people were present as senior girls from the north suburban school hazed their junior counterparts.

Officials at the Northbrook high school emphasized the game occurred off campus and without their knowledge.

Senior girls invited junior girls to participate in the event, even charging them

> I'm in high school and nothing like that happens around here! Why can't they just play the game?
> **Comparison**
> **Question**

money and supplying them with a T-shirt beforehand, officials said.

"It was hazing. It was deplorable treatment," said District 225 Supt. Dave Hales. "I guess there was some football involved, but then it was pushing, punching, hitting, putting buckets on heads . . . showering people with debris and, according to one report, human excrement." ●

School officials are cooperating with Cook County Forest Preserve District police in investigating the incident.

Hales said he was baffled why students participated in what appears to be a nonofficial tradition. The district in 1977 ended its annual powder-puff event during Homecoming because students had gotten too rough in their behavior.

"I think it gets carried over not as a school event, something we would never condone, by some small group of kids who think it's a rite of passage," Hales said.

"My question (to the students) is, where are your values? Where is your self-esteem? Why would you pay money to go to something where you know you will be treated inappropriately and humiliated and possibly injured?" ●

> I thought powderpuff was touch football, not beat each other and kick 'em when they're down! Those girls deserve a lot of punishment.
> **Opinion**
> **Judgment**

> Why would the girls go if they knew they were going to be tortured? I can't believe some people would go to see other people get humiliated.
> **Question**
> **Inserting Emotion—Shocked**

For the third modeling, recruit a student to think aloud as she reads while the rest of the class follows along and takes notes. It's important to show that thinking while reading is something that peers do as well as teachers. The following figures show how a newspaper article was used as the basis for a Think-Aloud and a list of skills that were gathered from a series of two Think-Alouds conducted with some juniors taking American literature.

Reading/Thinking Strategies

August 25	**August 29**
Relating to the story personally	Making a comparison
Questioning/wondering	Inserting emotion
Making inferences	Drawing conclusions
Making opinions	Making judgments
Media connection	Seeing a moral to the story
Visualizing/imagining	Connecting different parts of the text
	Making a historical connection

You've probably noticed that some of the thinking skills overlap. That's okay. Remember, the point is for the kids to start defining these reading skills, not you. If they think that "inserting emotion" is different from "relating to the story personally," then write it down!

Working the Room

The time to move around during this strategy is when the kids are working with their partners during each round. Make sure they understand that everyone should be prepared and have notes because you'll be calling on people at random.

Reflecting

After a few Think-Aloud modeling sessions, have another short piece ready for students to read silently. As in the texts that were modeled aloud, mark three or four dots where they should stop and jot down what they were thinking. Afterwards, have students look back at the list and write what kinds of thinking they were using. Students usually notice that they rely heavily on a few strategies. In their journals they should set goals for new thinking skills they will try to incorporate.

What Can Go Wrong?

The good news about this strategy is that it is pretty problem-free. The biggest consideration is which text to model. Make sure it is of high interest to teens, has some inherent puzzlement or controversy, and is not too long. Nothing kills a think-aloud faster than too much text. We've found that kids become antsy and bored with anything longer than two pages. Also, be sure students have adequate background knowledge so that confusion doesn't bog them down.

What's Next?

Think-Alouds are an excellent way to get kids to think more deeply about questions, connections, passages, and illustrations: the strategies they use when preparing for a literature circle discussion. Referring to previous Think-Aloud modeling also segues nicely into the strategy called Save the Last Word for Me, which is described in Chapter 5.

Written Conversation

Why Do It?

Kids love to write notes in school, right? Well, if you "legalize" this impulse and pull it into the curriculum, you've got a very powerful tool for interaction. When we are first preparing kids for book clubs, we often have them begin with *written*, rather than spoken, conversations. And we put them in pairs instead of larger groups, so that both members have heavy responsibility for the discussion. After kids have read a piece (short story, the first chapter of a novel, poem, cartoon, news article), the partners write short notes back and forth to each other about the reading. Using these pair conversations, you can have a "class discussion" where everyone is actively "talking" at once—though silently, in writing. Sure, some kids will drift off the topic or put down their pens after ten seconds, but most likely a solid majority of the class will be "conversing" about the reading. This activity is also known as dialogue or partner journals and is an integral feature of basic reading-writing workshop-style classrooms (Atwell 1998).

Teaching the Lesson

Getting Started

Assign or have students identify a partner for a written conversation. If you have an odd number of students, you can be a partner for the straggler. In this situation, we sometimes holler out, "Better hurry up and find a partner, because the last person left is gonna get *me!*" If you have an even number of students, that declaration guarantees everyone will find a partner fast. Or, let one group be a threesome—a trio can easily figure out how to trade back and forth.

Explain the activity by saying:

> *Members of each pair will write simultaneous notes to each other about the reading selection, swapping them every two or three minutes at my signal, for a total of three [or two or four] exchanges, and keeping quiet along the way. If you feel the urge to talk, write it down instead! These notes are supposed to be written like real, informal correspondence. Use greetings ("Dear Amy") and don't worry about spelling and grammar—after all, these are just notes. Pairs are to write for the whole time allotted for each note, putting down words, phrases, questions, connections, ideas, wonderings—anything related to the reading.*

You can leave the topic open ("whatever struck you about this reading") or remind kids to sample from the inventory of reading strategies, the different ways that smart readers think—connecting, questioning, predicting, noticing craft, evaluating, and all the rest.

Both students in each pair start writing a note (e.g., "Dear Janet, When I read this article, I was scared that global warming might be real . . ."). Meanwhile, watch the time, and after two or three minutes, say:

> *Finish the sentence you're on and don't forget to sign your name with a closing. Remember, these are supposed to be like letters. Once you've traded, read what your partner said, and then take two minutes to answer, just as if you were talking out loud. You can write responses, feelings, stories, make connections of your own, or ask your partner questions—anything you would do in a face-to-face conversation.*

After the planned two- or three-note exchange is complete, change the dynamic: "Okay, now you can talk out loud with your partner for a few minutes." You should notice a rising buzz in the room, showing that kids have plenty to talk about.

<u>North and South</u>

Dear Adam,
This book has a lot of similarities to <u>The Bastard</u> [another John Jakes book]. In both, the mothers die and the sons are out for revenge. Also, the stories start out in Europe and then the main characters want to journey to the colonies. Both characters learn a trade in Europe and then use it in the colonies. I think we'll meet this character's ~~stepfather's~~ family in America.

Mike

Dear Mike,
It seems like you know what you're talking about. I'm interested in what happens with Joseph since he's a slave now. I was wondering what happened to his mother after Joseph left. I think that Joe is going to be a very important character because he is going to fight in the Civil War as a slave. I also think that you are right about meeting Joseph's step-father's family in America. I would like to read the book <u>The Bastard</u>.

Adam

Dear Adam,

I think Joseph will also fight in the Civil War, not as a slave though. I think he'll fight on the North's side. He has the upper hand because he is white. Since he has to be a slave for seven years, he will fight to stop it. The Bastard is a pretty good book, except for the soap opera element. Some parts are pretty boring. It seems like every time someone is getting freaky, someone else interrupts.

Mike

Dear Mike,

Yes, you are right about Joe not being a slave. You are a very wise man. I would like to meet you someday. Do you think the Joe is going to live? What do you mean by getting freaky?

Adam

Dear Adam,

I think Joe will live through the whole book because he is a main character. You may very well someday be able to meet me. You will have to make arrangements with my secretary.

Mike

Working the Room

With Written Conversations, the teacher is very active. (And if you are part-nering with a student, you have even more to do.) You announce when each note starts and ends, usually two to three minutes per note. You want kids to write enough to spark a response but still keep the pace brisk. It helps if you wander through the room, looking over shoulders to see how much writing is occurring with each cycle (and also lending your "ministry of presence" to encourage on-task behavior). If you notice that kids have already written a lot, you might call time earlier; if they are slower, you could let them go an-other minute. You also need to call out instructions: "Okay, in thirty seconds, we're going to stop writing and exchange notes, so you might want to end the sentence you're working on right now." Then a few seconds later you might say: "Just throw a period down there somewhere. We're going to stop and swap now."

Reflecting

Finish up with a short whole-class discussion. You'll find that this sharing is often quite engaging and energetic because everyone will have fresh ideas about the topic. Ask a few pairs to share one highlight or one thread of their written conversations that really sparked their partner to think and write back. Brainstorming a quick list of the strategies students used to prod their partners into an extended written dialogue will improve the next round of journaling as well as help the students who put their pens down early. Inter-estingly, the sample list shown pretty much describes what should happen during a literature circle meeting as well.

What Can Go Wrong?

When notes are passed, the kids will tend to shift into oral conversation (adults do this also—it's a normal human response when you are bonding with a partner). Be ready to remind them to "keep it in writing" during the transitions.

Even with the best instructions, some kids will write two words and put their pens down, wasting lots of good writing time with each pass. Keep

Helpful Written Conversation Strategies

Pay attention to what the other person is saying/writing

Give opinions and back them up

Use examples

Expand on your ideas

Say funny stuff

Connect your own experiences to the reading

Ask a lot of questions

Answer your partner's questions with a lot of detail

Come up with interesting ideas

Use the characters' names

Make predictions

Express feelings

Say how the reading relates to the real world

Keep the conversation going by bringing up a new topic—
don't repeat the same thing over and over

Argue and disagree, but in a nice way

Talk about what you think is important

Use your imagination

Refer to specific scenes/incidents

Comment on your partner's ideas/opinions

Use a lot of details

---

stressing that "we write for the whole time" and use your debriefing time to address this problem.

Once in a while, a pair will get sidetracked when they decide the text is boring (as you can see in the This Book Is Boring exchange). Catching these straying conversations early will allow you to help students redirect their reading/thinking strategies before it is too late.

With Jeff and Kaitlin, who were reading *Across Five Aprils*, quick intervention was in order. When Nancy talked to the kids, they were having some trouble keeping all of the characters straight. They were also frustrated because "nothing was happening." This was a book about the Civil War, but there weren't any battles. Once the students understood that this was a war

Dear Kaitlin,
So far I am not liking this book. I have no idea
of what's going on. I'm not seeing a conflict or
something happening in the book yet. I hope it
will get a lot better as I read on. So far it is very
dull and boring. The author writes just like how
they talk in the South. Maybe it will be more
interesting when I get to the battle scenes that
have lots of action.
Jeff

Dear Jeff,
I agree. I thought the book was very boring at
the beginning and it was kind of hard to determine
what they were saying by the accents they
talked with. I think after they are done with
the first chapter and introducing everyone, it will
get more interesting. I also think there will
be more battle scenes after awhile too.
Kaitlin

Dear Kaitlin,
Maybe the next chapter will have more action and
conflict. Hopefully it will make more sense and
will be easier to understand.
Jeff

Dear Jeff,
Yes, I hope there will be something that happens
because it's so boring right now with nothing
going on. Maybe we can look forward to some
exciting war scenes, but I doubt it with
reading the first few pages. This book is just
so boring and I dont see any climax coming.
Kaitlin

story about the parents, spouses, and children who were worrying about the safety of family members in combat, their attitude toward the book changed because they began reading it with a completely different set of expectations and predictions. In the end, they all enjoyed the book.

In the worst-case scenario, some students, especially boys, will follow completely inappropriate tangents in the name of humor. Two gentlemen in Nancy's class once ended up explaining their rather graphic journals to the boys' dean; he was not impressed. It never hurts to remind the class, "Anything you write in these conversations needs to be G rated, suitable for all audience members; that includes me and your parents. If you're not sure whether something is appropriate, save it for passing period when you can talk about it on your own time."

Finally, once the kids are talking out loud with their partners, you may find it very hard to call them back to order. This happy little "management problem" shows you that kids are connecting to each other and the material. But you still may have to yell to get their attention.

Variations

Skip the two-minute drill and let kids find their own timing, their own writing-and-reading rhythm, as long as they keep writing.

After a few notes and swaps between pairs, put two or three pairs together for an out-loud conversation, using their written conversations as a source of topics.

3

Practicing with Short Text: Tools for Thoughtful Response

The main idea behind literature circles is for students to choose interesting books and have thoughtful peer-led conversations about them. But teachers often (and rightfully) worry: "What if the kids don't remember enough to sustain a twenty- or thirty-minute discussion? What if I send my students off to their book clubs and they sit there staring at each other with nothing to say?" Yikes—we can't have that! We need kids to arrive at their discussions with plenty to talk about.

How do adult readers avoid this problem in their reading groups? If you visit a few such clubs, you'll notice that veteran readers possess specific strategies for capturing responses while they read and tools for flagging particular passages they want to talk about later. Some readers put marks or words in the margins; others underline or circle passages; others fold over a page corner to mark an important section. Our friend Yolanda really attacks the text, highlighting the passages related to each character in a different color (yellow for Atticus, pink for Dill, blue for Jem, etc.). Today, many readers use sticky notes to jot ideas beside an important passage without spoiling the page (especially appropriate for library or borrowed books). Some lucky readers are able to harvest their responses mentally, needing no physical annotations to refresh their memories when a book discussion starts. We don't know if this is a sign of literary maturity or just a learning-style difference, but few people—and certainly neither of us—can operate without some kind of memory crutch.

So what about our students? How can we help them to remember their most important responses? We know what you might be thinking: Your students can run their eyes over a book and then remember nothing a day (or an hour) later. No matter what we might think in our lowest moments (say, right after that seventh-period class on the Wednesday before Thanksgiving), our students *do* have responses while they read. They have feelings, questions, pictures in their minds; they do make predictions, judge characters and authors. The trouble is, they may lack strategies for capturing those responses before they evaporate.

That's why it is so important, early in the life of your classroom book clubs, to teach students a repertoire of strategies for captivating and recording their

- feelings
- visualizations
- connections
- predictions
- questions
- judgments
- inferences
- responses

This chapter introduces six different tools to help students surface and record all these reading responses.

Each of the devices works at multiple levels. First, simply approaching material with a tool in hand reminds students to enter the text thinking, to be conscious of their responses as they read. Second, each tool invites students to stop, either during or after reading, and immediately record their thinking, before it can be overwritten by the biology homework or a late-night TV movie. Third, all the notes, in whatever form, travel to the next book club meeting where they refresh students' memories and become a seedbed of discussion possibilities for everyone.

When first trying literature circles in your classroom, you may be tempted to "be sure kids have plenty to talk about" by handing out your own list of discussion questions. By doing this, of course, you are encouraging kids to be dependent on *you* for conversation topics, instead of taking the responsibility themselves. Plus, if you distribute teacher-generated questions, you're likely to see shallow, mechanical meetings, focused on getting the right answer for you, and not the lively, free-flowing conversations that are the hallmark of genuine book clubs.

Smart teachers introduce just one or two of the following devices in the first book club cycle. They usually pick the ones that seem best fitted to their students. If your kids need a lot of structure, start with the role sheets; if you want to encourage extended written responses, try journal writing. But don't overdo it; one or two of these tools will be plenty to equip kids for tackling a book. Later you can gradually introduce the others as variations or fresh approaches.

The structure of these six mini-lessons is simple and similar: You introduce the tool; the kids read a short text using the tool; the students meet with a partner or small group for a quick discussion (five to ten minutes); and finally, you hold a whole-class debriefing about how the tool helped to feed good discussion. As we'll reiterate throughout the chapter, kids can try these new techniques on a wide range of short texts, including:

- a section from a novel
- a short-short story
- a graph or chart

- a poem

- a news article

- a selection from a trade nonfiction book

It also helps to show examples of effectively completed notes, sheets, or journals, using handouts or overhead transparencies, so students know what good work looks like.

Because these six tools and the corresponding mini-lessons are somewhat similar, we've kept the descriptions extra short. We give a bit more time to role sheets, since they are a popular but tricky little device, but just a stream-lined introduction and illustration of the other five.

Teachers sometimes wonder: Do my students need to use one or another note-taking strategy forever, with everything they read? Well, how do successful lifelong readers operate? In adult book clubs, some individuals can be effective discussants without any written notes, while others need something tangible to refer to. If we are going to respect different learning and thinking styles, we should eventually let kids find their own natural way of operating. The proof is in the conversations, not on paper; if kids can join in lively discussions without notes, why not let them? But let's train them carefully first; then they have the tools if they need them.

Role Sheets

Why Do It?

In the early days of literature circles—the late eighties and early nineties, if you can remember that far back—most of us used "role sheets" with our student book clubs. These tools had catchy titles like Discussion Director, Connector, Literary Luminary, Illustrator, and Vocabulary Enricher. The task definitions gave each participant a different job to do, both while reading and while discussing. Each role sheet helped students notice and capture important ideas while reading and provided a structured written form to bring to the next book club meeting.

The idea of using an array of tasks traces back to the general principles of good collaborative learning, specifically the idea of individual and group accountability. When we started doing book clubs, we wanted to adapt the idea of cooperative group roles to reading discussions, but didn't want to use empty generic roles like "encourager," "record keeper," or "process checker." So instead, we built roles out of the different cognitive strategies that smart readers use:

Role	Reading Strategy
Discussion Director	asking questions
Connector	making connections
Illustrator	visualizing
Vocabulary Enricher	noticing author's craft
Literary Luminary	determining importance

The roles were theoretically sound, both from a reading-as-thinking point of view and as an embodiment of well-structured collaborative learning.

The problem was that the sheets got mixed results. While they worked for the initial training of groups (and helped kids to recognize how smart readers think), they later tended to evoke mechanical, pro forma discussions rather than the sparkling conversation we desire in literature circles. When teachers clung to the sheets for longer than a brief training period, the roles often boomeranged, stifling discussions rather than energizing them. We've learned a lot about role sheets since those days, and one of our best new understandings is embodied in this mini-lesson. If you don't divide up the roles, but give all the readers the same three or four jobs, the sheets work much better.

Teaching the Lesson

Getting Started

Provide each student with a blank role sheet. You can make your own custom version, including any two to four thinking strategies you want to stress, or use the form shown on the next page. This particular example encourages readers to be alert for four important kinds of response: determining importance, making personal connections, noticing the author's craft, and asking questions. Give students a few moments to read the sheet carefully and then check to be sure everyone understands the four jobs. Once the tasks are clear, pass out a piece of short text and ask students to make notes in each of the four categories, either while they read or just after they finish. Allow five minutes for the reading and writing.

Now have students form groups—pairs if you want high social pressure with minimum craziness, threes or fours if the class is reasonably adept socially. Tell the kids to have "a nice conversation" for about five minutes, using their notes as they wish, and talk about wherever the story took them. If you fear that kids will cling too closely to their notes and thus inhibit a free-flowing conversation, give them this option: "Put your role sheets face down on the desk, and just look at the story instead and talk it over. If you run out of things to talk about, you can flip the sheets over, remind yourselves of another idea to discuss, and then turn them face down again."

Multiple Role Sheet: Short Story

Passages: Please mark any words, lines, or sections of the story that "stick out" for you. These passages might be important, puzzling, curious, provocative, dubious, or well written—whatever grabs your attention.

Reactions/Connections: What were your feelings and responses to this story? Did it remind you of past experiences, people, or events in your life? Did it make you think of anything happening in the news, around school, in other stories or books you have read?

Craft: What did you notice about the author's style, language, point of view, literary devices, or structures she/he used to create the story?

Questions: What questions came to mind while you were reading this story? Were there things you wondered about, doubted, or didn't understand? What would you ask the author or the characters if you could talk to them?

Working the Room

Walk around and observe the groups at work. The conversation may seem a bit artificial at first, but probably the kids will have plenty to talk about. If you spot a group that's struggling, sit with them briefly, either just to listen or to ask: "What's going wrong?"

Reflecting

When we do these short training exercises, we always want to put the literature—the story and the ideas—first, before we debrief the process. So, begin by asking several groups to share a "highlight of the conversation"—one topic that they discussed at length, argued over, or laughed about. Ask what conversations were sparked by a particular job on the role sheet. "Did anyone talk about some passages that seemed especially important?" If they tried the face-down version, ask how well kids remembered what they had written. Our experience, confirmed by a lot of students, is that once you have jotted down a response, you tend to recall it when you look at the text, whether you have your notes in front of you or not. That's what we call writing-to-learn!

You can also ask the students directly how they liked the role sheets and how the tool worked for them as readers and group members. This might lead kids to redesign the sheets after using them once or twice. The more ownership we can develop for these or any other tools, the more likely they are to support careful reading and enthusiastic discussion.

What Can Go Wrong?

Of the six response-harvesting strategies presented here, role sheets are probably the most structured. They are especially good for teaching or reinforcing the ways smart readers think, and they are infinitely adaptable to different genres and texts. But no matter how cleverly you design them, role sheets always look a lot like worksheets, and they can inadvertently activate the disengaged, let's-get-it-over-with attitude that students often bring to such tasks. You'll recognize this problem if you see kids mechanically going around their circle with no cross-talk or interaction, wearily reporting in sequence: "Here's my passage, here's my connection, here's my picture, here's my author's craft."

This dulling response seems to escalate the longer you use role sheets. That's why we usually recommend using them only for a brief initial training period (or to spice up a lesson later on), and then moving on to one or more of the more open-ended tools on the following pages.

Response Logs

Why Do It?

One of the most natural and open-ended ways for a reader to capture her own responses is to keep a personal log or journal. In this special space, the owner can range freely through all the different kinds of thinking that smart readers do as well as choose the best format (words, phrases, lists, sentences, paragraphs, doodles, diagrams, charts) to capture the ideas. Once kids know all the different ways that proficient readers respond, we want them to use the medium that fits best rather than be constrained by a mandated list or format.

For this kind of open-ended thinking and collecting, response logs are a great tool. You can have kids do this writing in the literature circle journals we recommended in Chapter 1. You remember, the journals they use for taking careful notes during your mini-lessons? If you go this route, help kids develop clear-cut headings or sections so the various types of entries are quickly accessible. Remember, though, we are in the midst of introducing five *other* ways of capturing and storing reading responses. Journals definitely do not have to do double duty. You can "keep shopping" until you find the best one or two harvesting tools for your kids.

In many schools, reading response logs are already in widespread use, and some high school teachers receive new ninth-graders who have been journaling for years. To them, logs are a major "duh." We should all thank Nancie Atwell, more than anyone else, for this happy development (1998). If you're lucky enough to have such veteran journal writers in your class, you're off and running. But if your students don't know a response log from a lab manual, it's a great time to teach it.

Teaching the Lesson

Getting Started

Introduce the idea of a reading response log by showing some good examples on overhead transparencies. These can be student samples from previous classes or logs you have created yourself. The examples will be most effective if the students are familiar with the text—perhaps a novel they recently read as a class. Next, you can do a "log-aloud," where you hand out a short article and have everyone read it together. Then *you* compose a response log entry on the blackboard or on a blank transparency, talking as you go and modeling how a skilled reader notices her thinking and jots down its essence. (See the Think-Aloud mini-lesson in Chapter 2 for more on this kind of teacher modeling.) Often, this demonstration will lead you back to that familiar list of things that smart readers attend to: questions, predictions, inferences, connections, visualizations, and issues of craft (see page 9).

Now it's time for the students to try some journal writing on their own. They can use their already-established lit circle journals, regular notebook paper, or a special journal just for these reading notes. If you choose the latter, give kids a few days to find a special format that will work for them. Choosing one's own journal can be unique and idiosyncratic; it's part of the ritual—and the lure. Before kids dive into this practice session, reiterate the different kinds of thinking smart readers do and the wide range of formats journalers may use.

Now hand out another short piece. We've often used the example shown in this lesson—a chart from a newspaper article. When students are just starting to use response logs, you might say:

Read the article, and then write for two minutes nonstop. Write whatever's in your mind, wherever your reading is taking you. Remember all your choices [point to the poster of reading strategies in the front of the room]. You can write your feelings, reactions, questions, opinions;

you can draw or diagram your ideas; you can talk about the author's style and strategies. But you must keep writing for the whole two minutes—no fair writing down one or two words and putting your pen down.

When kids have finished the reading and writing, have them join in small groups (two to four people) for short (five-minute) discussions of the article. Encourage students to use the notes however they help, but mainly to have a "natural, friendly conversation."

Working the Room

While kids are writing in their response logs, circulate and look over shoulders. If you see students with blank pages, sit next to them, quietly ask what's up, and offer help or suggestions. You may need to target these strugglers with a later conference or written conversation to help them grasp the idea. If you see kids with great logs, get permission to copy them as examples for the next class, or for other classes you teach.

When students switch to group discussion time, sit for one minute in each group to get a flavor of what's happening across the whole class. Probably, you'll see groups finding plenty to discuss, with no more than occasional glances at the logs. This is good; it means that the writing has helped kids to develop a mental inventory of topics to address in their groups. After three to five minutes, call time and ask groups to share the highlights from their conversations. As always, we honor the literature by talking content first and process later.

Reflecting

Ask kids to talk about how the journaling worked and what changes could make it a more effective tool for both reading and meeting. If necessary, do another practice session or two. That's it.

Sample Selection for Response Log Practice

City's victims, killers have much in common

In the first six months of 2003, there were 288 homicides citywide, a pace that, if continued, would make this year the first since 1968 in which there were fewer than 600 homicides in Chicago.

OFFENDER/VICTIM COMPARISON*
(January–June 2003)

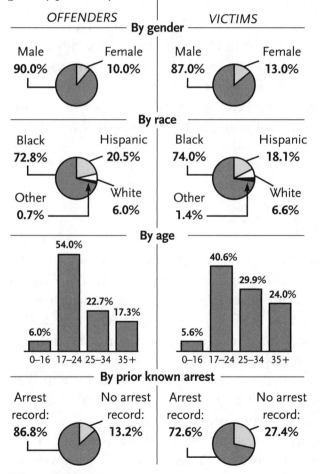

OFFENDERS   VICTIMS

By gender

| Male 90.0% | Female 10.0% | Male 87.0% | Female 13.0% |

By race

| Black 72.8% | Hispanic 20.5% | Black 74.0% | Hispanic 18.1% |
| Other 0.7% | White 6.0% | Other 1.4% | White 6.6% |

By age

OFFENDERS: 6.0% (0–16), 54.0% (17–24), 22.7% (25–34), 17.3% (35+)

VICTIMS: 5.6% (0–16), 40.6% (17–24), 29.9% (25–34), 24.0% (35+)

By prior known arrest

| Arrest record: 86.8% | No arrest record: 13.2% | Arrest record: 72.6% | No arrest record: 27.4% |

*Where offender is known.

Source: Chicago Police Department. Copyright 2003 Chicago Tribune Company. All rights reserved. Used with permission.

Sample Student Response Log

I was surprised to hear that there were "only" 288 murders in Chicago this year so far. I mean on the news it seems like there are millions of people shooting each other every day! I wasn't that surprised about men being the biggest murderers, much more than women—you hardly ever hear about women being killers—or when you do, they make a big deal out of it.

The statistics I guess are showing who really kills who in Chicago, which is black and Hispanic people killing each other, and it's mostly younger men that are doing it. So this makes me think one thing: gangs, that must be where a lot of this goes on. In a way these statistics make the city look terrible and dangerous, but you think, well, maybe where you live there might not be any murders at all, depending on who lives in your neighborhood.

So, the pie chart really shocked me—most of the killers *and* the victims have been in trouble with the law before. Maybe if we kept them all locked up?

What Can Go Wrong?

The only problems with journals are pretty minor. One is that they are separate from the books kids are reading, unlike sticky notes, text coding, or bookmarks, which by definition are placed *inside the book*. So logs are one more thing for kids to keep track of ("It's in my locker, honest!"). In discussions, kids can fumble and lose focus trying to correlate journal entries with the right section of the book. To solve this problem, we always ask kids to jot page numbers beside key journal entries they are planning to raise in their group. For kids who struggle with writing, a big blank journal page may cause more "composition anxiety" than a tiny sticky note or blank area on a role sheet. But as long as we are clear about the standards (words, phrases, lists, or doodles are okay; response logs aren't supposed to be essays), even the fearful can adjust.

Post-its

Why Do It?

We sometimes wonder how literate people managed before that scientist in St. Paul, Minnesota, accidentally invented Post-it notes. For readers who want to jot down ideas and mark things in books or magazines, there's no better tool. They come in all sizes, shapes, and colors (and now, of course, from countless manufacturers). You can place them right at the spot where you want to return, with the edge sticking out so they're easy to find. Then when you're done, you just remove all the notes and return the book to its virgin state, ready for the next reader. In our classes, we collect those notes when students finish a book. If you stick them in page-number order on plain paper, you have a record of the student's thinking all the way through a book. Slap the notes in the kid's portfolio: instant assessment!

In our own teaching, Post-its have really become the baseline harvesting tool. Take a look at Tegan's Sticky Notes from *Huckleberry Finn.* As you read over this example, just imagine the four other students in her book club bringing even more responses to share—you can tell this literature circle will have plenty to discuss. You may also notice that Tegan writes a first line about what's happening on this page, so when she later moves the note from the book to her journal or portfolio, she will remember what was happening where this note was placed.

Tegan's Sticky Notes from *Huckleberry Finn*

Huck Finn
Pages 68–130

Tegan
November 19, 2003
2nd Hour

Questions	Passages
Page 74 Who was making the whooping noise? Is it Indians? Will Huck find what is making the noise? Will it hurt him?	Page 77 Huck lied to Jim about the whooping and the raft floating away. He apologized to a black person. Why did he tell Jim the truth afterall? Why did he lie at first? Will Jim be angry at Huck?
Page 78 Will they ever find Cairo? Where is Cairo? Will they settle there? What will they do if they get there?	Page 85 When the steamboat split the raft in half forcing Jim and Huck into the water. Will Jim be alright? Will he die? Will Huck save him?
Page 97 Why did he shoot at the man? What was the feud about? Will anyone die? Has anyone already been killed?	Page 101 When Huck and Jim see each other again, Jim says he fixed the raft and that it wasn't theirs that got smashed. How did Jim find the raft? What did he use to fix it? How long were they separated?
Page 112 Where was the Duke from? Where was the King from? Will Jim and Huck let them stay long? What will they get in return?	Page 104 When Buck and other family members died over the feud. Why didn't they care if they died? What would happen if Huck died? Would Huck be injured?
Page 116 Will Jim be able to travel during the day? What is the plan? Will it work? Will Jim get into trouble if they try the plan?	Page 123 When everyone was practicing for the play and got it down very well. Would they ever perform it for anyone? Would everyone be in it? Will they make any money from it?

Connections:
Jim and Huck were talking about snake skin as bad luck. I walked under a ladder and had bad luck for a whole week. P84
Huck is trying to cover up his mistake and lie to Jim. I have done something similar to my mom before. P76

Teaching the Lesson

Getting Started

As with all the other harvesting strategies, the goal is to show students how this tool can work for them, let them practice it with short texts and brief discussions, and then turn them loose on full-length books. The best way to begin, as always, is to show how you use the tool yourself. Make photocopies or transparencies of a selection of your own sticky notes, ideally from a book that students have also read. Copy the whole book page with the note hanging off the edge, so you can demonstrate how the note related to a specific section of text. You can also do a "Post-Aloud" demonstration, where you put a page of text on the overhead and then show kids how you'd flag one or two items on that page.

Next it's time for some Post-it practice. Start each student with a finite number of Post-its (say three) and a one-page story or article to read. Remind them that these notes, as you have just demonstrated, can be used to capture the same things they might write in a journal or on a role sheet (feelings, predictions, connections, questions, visualizations, reactions, judgments). But instead, they write on a series of notes as they read, placing them right next to text they want to return to later. Have kids read the article and write their notes. Then place them briefly in discussion groups, using the notes as a source of topics.

Working the Room

As usual, circulate to make sure kids are on task, to solve problems, and to dole out more sticky notes if needed.

Reflecting

After kids have met for at least five minutes, invite them to share highlights from the discussion; what were the big ideas they talked about? Then shift to debriefing the logistics of Post-it use: "How well did this tool work? How does it differ from a journal or a role sheet? What's your comfort level—do you like this format or do you prefer another harvesting tool? Why?" If more practice is needed, repeat with other short texts.

What Can Go Wrong?

When we turn kids loose with Post-its, there is often an adjustment period. Kids may vastly overuse the notes, plastering them all over every page. Some notes will contain few or no comments, raising questions about exactly what is being marked for later discussion. A mini-lesson on focus and selectivity might be in order. At other times, kids may hesitate to "spend" a note, agonizing too much about whether a given response is worthy. This can be a cue that more teacher modeling is needed—perhaps another "Post-Aloud" mini-lesson.

One other problem that occurs with almost every harvesting tool is coverage. Particularly when given a quota (e.g., "you need to have six Post-its for the next discussion"), some kids will follow the letter of the law rather than the spirit. When we notice that all of the notes are located on the first six pages of the reading and none are left for the other seventy pages, it's time to have a quick discussion of what we call "spread." We say: "When you come to a discussion, your notes need to reflect all of the reading rather than a small portion of it. If you have more stickies than the required number, that's okay. That gives you the opportunity to look them over and pick your best ideas to use in the discussion."

time 20 needed

Bookmarks

Why Use It?

There's nothing more traditional and useful than a bookmark, a talisman that travels with you through the pages of your reading adventure. The trouble is, most bookmarks are small and made of stuff you can't write on—plastic, leather, even metal. But if you make a bookmark of paper, then it can do more than mark your place in the text; it can become a multipurpose tool for recording your thinking as you go, a storage system for ideas to share with your book club later on.

This tool works only with books—you can't use it with one-page stories, for obvious reasons. You can introduce this strategy just before your students start a new round of book clubs, or in the middle of a literature circle cycle as a new way of capturing responses in a book.

Teaching the Lesson

Getting Started

Introduce the idea by showing samples of effective bookmarks from books that kids know. These could be bookmarks made by previous students or specimens you have created in advance. Even better, model how you would make a bookmark yourself by writing on the blackboard or an overhead transparency as you "read" through a section of book that students have in front of them. You could also photocopy a sample bookmark and have students study it alongside the book section it refers to.

Once you've explained and modeled the idea, it's time for kids to make their own bookmarks. Have your students take out a piece of regular notebook paper and fold it in thirds lengthwise. When folded, this yields a plausibly bookmark-shaped item about three by eleven inches, with two sides to write on. If you divide each panel in half horizontally, you get four nice-sized blank spaces for jotting notes.

You or the students can decide what type of responses might go in each quadrant. You can draw on that familiar list (questions, connections, craft items, etc.) or choose other topics that fit a particular book well. Look at the bookmark Ariana made when she was reading the nonfiction best-seller *Fast Food Nation* by Eric Schlosser. As you can see from her bookmark, the four chosen categories were

1. Personal responses

2. Important passages

3. Questions

4. Important statistics

Notice the wide range of thinking Ariana collected—from personal reactions and questions to key passages and statistics. When her group gets to this section of *Fast Food Nation*, you know they'll have lots to discuss.

Ask the kids to help make a list of four topics that would be appropriate for the range of books they are currently reading in their book clubs. Have them meet in their clubs for two or three minutes to come up with suggestions. Then bring everyone back for a quick consensus-building meeting. Pick out four clear and distinctly different items you could track with a bookmark. There's no such thing as four "correct" ones; let kids play around with whatever topics they suggest.

Working the Room

Now put the kids to work. Ask them to develop a simple "practice bookmark" for the section of the book they will be discussing in their next book club meeting. This means they are working with some chapters they have already read and are prepared to discuss. As they create their bookmarks, students will obviously be drawing partly on other notes they had made for the

Student Bookmark for *Fast Food Nation*

Front	*fold*	Back

Front

"Fast Food Nation"

<u>Response</u>

  I think it's very unfair how most fast food restaurant employees get treated. I never realized that f.f. restaurants don't have unions. I also think it's true that managers use "stroking" to bring confidence to their employees instead of highering their wages

<u>Important passage</u>

  Long hours many American teenagers now spend on the job pose a great risk to their future educational & financial success. Kids who work up to 20 hrs. a week during the school year benefit from the experience, gaining responsibility & self-esteem. But kids who work more than that are likely to cut classes & drop out.

Back

<u>Questions</u>

- I don't really understand how the tax act works on restaurants.

- Why doesn't the government enforce laws so that employ can form their unior

<u>Important Quotes</u>

- " Teenagers are far more likely to be untrained, and every year, about 200,000 are injured on the job pg. 83

- "Many of the customers look down on fast food workers & feel entitled to treat the with disrespect." pg. 81

day's discussion, whether journal entries or sticky notes. In a sense, they'll simply be transferring some ideas to another format. But they'll also have to come up with all four kinds of response that the bookmark requires. Finally, have kids take these bookmarks right into their next book club meetings and try them out.

....

Reflecting

At debriefing time, ask students to write in their journals or talk about how the bookmarks supported their discussions, compared to the other tools used to date. Push them to look closely at each of the assigned categories: "Which ones generated the best discussions in your group? Which ones did you use the least? What new categories could you test out?"

What Can Go Wrong?

We find bookmarks to be a pretty bullet-proof strategy. They work well with all kinds of books, especially the adult nonfiction trade books that are a growing part of our students' reading diets. The physical limitation of writing space gives kids a comfortable, not-too-much, not-too-little standard to work with. The only real problem comes if the teacher dictates uninspiring or onerous categories for the notes. Watch out for a steep attitudinal drop-off if you command kids to record metaphors, prepositions, or relative clauses on their bookmarks.

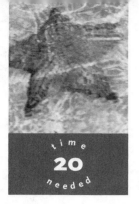

time
20
needed

Drawing

Why Do It?

We teachers often complain that kids today watch too much television, play too many video games, and are flooded with ready-made visual images everywhere they turn. We also notice that many of these overstimulated kids can't make pictures in their own heads while reading a book. Indeed, their inability to create vivid sensory images may be one reason that so many kids will throw down a perfectly wonderful book, saying: "This is boring." We're not sure of all the causes for this affliction, but it does seem like our young people need some remedial visualization experiences, some encouragement and practice with creating sensory images as they read.

Drawing, charting, mapping, and other forms of graphic response also serve the range of learning styles that exist in any real classroom. Too often, we confine students' literary responses to written or spoken language, even though we know that some of our own most powerful responses to a book come from a vision of the place, our image of a character, or the picture we make of a single stunning moment. Many times, a drawn or graphic response can capture those elements better than more words.

Occasionally, we'll have students use drawing or mapping as their main harvesting strategy for an article or book. But more often, we invite them to use drawing as one of several tools: as one job on a role sheet, one quadrant of a bookmark, one thing you can put on a sticky note, or another kind of journal entry.

Teaching the Lesson

....

Getting Started

The secret to introducing drawing as a response tool is to not evoke everyone's art phobia. Young people, just like many of us adults, tend to feel that art is a hereditary talent unfairly distributed among the population—and which has not graced their DNA. So we introduce this lesson in this way:

> *Today we're going to use a new tool for capturing our responses while we read, for recording ideas to talk over in our book clubs. Instead of jotting down words, we're going to respond graphically—meaning we're going to draw something. Now, don't worry—this is not an art lesson. We're talking about simple sketching, cartooning, even stick figure drawings. It's not about who makes the prettiest picture, but about using this form to capture something important or special about your book and your thinking.*

Modeling by the teacher is especially important for the success of this tool, and a key mini-lesson step is to do a "draw-aloud." Have the class read a short piece of text; then draw your own graphic response on the chalkboard or an overhead transparency. Vocalize as you draw:

> *When I was reading the prologue to Maniac McGee, I was really struck by the poem, that jump-rope rhyme—'Maniac, Maniac, he's so cool'—and the part where he kissed the bull. So I'm drawing Maniac here, and now here's the bull, who I thought would be really big and angry, so I'm drawing him snorting from his nostrils . . .*

Now it's the kids' turn. Pass out a short-short story, poem, or news clipping, and say:

> *After you've finished the reading, take a couple of minutes to draw a response to what you've just read. You can do any kind of drawing you like:*

- *A scene, character, moment, or event from the story*

- *An image or picture that came to mind while you were reading; it could be a memory or scene from your life*

- *A diagram, flow chart, or map of the story*

- *An abstract form that represents a thought or feeling you got from the reading—an explosion, a thunderbolt, a pattern, etc.*

Remember, this is not an art lesson, it's not about drawing talent, and it is not for a grade. This is just another way of remembering what strikes you when you read. We're going to draw this really fast, so you won't have time to worry or hesitate.

Give some time for individual drawing. Then place kids in groups of three or four and invite them to have a short discussion of the text, using these instructions as a guide:

One good way to use your drawings is to take turns showing your picture to the group. Don't say anything at first—let the other kids try to guess what you were representing in the picture. When everyone has had a chance to comment, then you can tell people what your picture was about.

Working the Room

While students are drawing, quietly walk around, helping any kids who have gone blank or are having an artistic panic attack. Usually the job is just to remind them of all the different kinds of "drawing" they might use for this assignment, or to help them pick out one thing to work with. If we run across a kid who's genuinely struggling with the art thing, to be merciful, we'll just assign a story event for the student to draw. If we see one of the jokesters developing a drawing that will exceed a PG rating, we quietly invoke the Mother Rule (Don't do anything in here that wouldn't make your mother proud).

Reflecting

You can spark a great follow-up discussion with a "gallery walk." Have kids tape their drawings to the wall at eye-level height, at three-foot intervals all around the classroom. Invite everyone to stroll through the gallery of drawn reading responses. Then have kids sit back down and ask them: "Who can tell us about a picture that started some really good conversation in your group?" Have the volunteers stand beside the picture they're commenting on and explain specifically what good talk the picture sparked, and how. Often, it's not the literal pictures that generated discussion, but the more high-concept models and designs. A bonus to this activity: Because drawing invokes other part of the brain, another learning style, a different set of kids often gets singled out for their good work.

What Can Go Wrong?

Once you get past the initial anxiety or foreignness, drawing usually becomes a popular part of the reading response repertoire. Sometimes, too popular. Some kids will cleave to drawing to the exclusion of other forms of response. They may think that drawing a picture is "easier" or less onerous than writing down words, words, words. As long as students can base productive, thoughtful, small-group discussions on pictures, we choose not to see this as a problem. But some teachers we know have had to make rules: "You can't only draw pictures about this book; you've got to have at least some notes every day." Your choice.

Juliet's Soliloquy

> What if this mixture do not work at all?
> Shall I be married then tomorrow morning?
> No, no, this shall forbid it. Lie thou there.
> What if it be a poison that the Friar
> Subtly hath ministered to have me dead,
> Lest in this marriage he be dishonored
> Because he married me before to Romeo? . . .
> How if, when I'm laid in the tomb,
> I wake before the time that Romeo
> Come to redeem me? There's a fearful point.
> Shall I not then be stifled in the vault . . .
> Where for this many hundred years the bones
> Of all my buried ancestors are packed; . . .
> O, if I wake, shall I not be distraught,
> Environed with all these hideous fears,
> And madly play with my forefathers' joints,
> And pluck the mangled Tybalt from his shroud,
> And in this rage, with some great kinsman's bone,
> As with a club dash out my des'prate brains? . . .

William Shakespeare, *Romeo and Juliet*, Act 4, Scene 3, lines 25–60.

Walter's Illustration

If you're worried that your students will be overwhelmed by the openness of the basic task, narrow it down: "Pick one line or sentence that really struck you in the reading. Do your drawing about that, and copy the words from the book right under your picture."

Illustrations often encourage students to examine the text more closely. When reading Act 4 of *Romeo and Juliet,* Walter chose to depict the apprehension Juliet expresses in the soliloquy she delivers just before taking Friar Lawrence's potion.

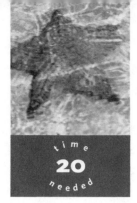

Text Coding

Why Do It?

Proficient readers often have ways of marking or coding text they want to re-member. Maybe they use a yellow highlighter, underline or box words, or put marks in the margins to flag questions, exclamations, or wonderment as they read. Indeed, marking up the text may be the most simple, practical, and widespread harvesting tool that regular readers use. In school, however, students are often discouraged from making any marks in their books. In fact, the more challenging the material (like science or history textbooks), the less likely that kids will be allowed to use this effective tool for enhancing comprehension. Too bad.

When books or other materials *can* be marked up, it's important for students to have a useful set of response codes. This is especially helpful with dense, content-loaded texts where every single word matters, like poetry or fact-filled nonfiction books. When addressing such tough text, students need to attack the page, penetrate the surface, and dig out the meaning with very active strategies. For example, when our students read *Fast Food Nation*, which is a lively but really hard book, the kids used a version of a text-marking system called the Interactive Notation System for Effective Reading and Thinking (INSERT). Along with coding, we encouraged them to jot words or phrases in the margins as another way of flagging big ideas, strong reactions, or puzzling questions.

For this mini-lesson, we use the INSERT system as modified by the students at Best Practice High School in Chicago. However, we encourage you to

INSERT Codes for Taking Notes

INSERT (Best Practice High School Variation)

If a section:

- ✓ Confirms what you thought
- ✗ Contradicts what you thought
- ? Raises a question
- ?? Confuses you
- ★ Seems important
- ! Is new or interesting

If a word

Gets repeated
Seems important
Is unknown

Box it: | Word |

invent a set of response codes with your students. That's a great mini-lesson in itself.

Teaching the Lesson

Getting Started

Hand out a copy of the INSERT system and review all the codes with students. Invite them to add new ones if they have ideas for symbols to represent other kinds of important responses. Next do a quick teacher demonstration, marking up a short story or article you have put on an overhead transparency. As always, vocalize your thinking process as you model marking the text: "Well, I already knew that." [checkmark] "What? I don't understand this." [question mark] "Now that's really important." [exclamation point]

Then hand out a different short text and invite kids to try out the marking system for themselves.

In coding the following Edgar Allan Poe poem, students were encouraged to use both the text-marking system and marginal words or phrases to help them explore the text.

Working the Room

Make your normal rounds, observing how kids are putting the codes to work and helping if asked for clarifications. You'll probably notice highly variable code use; some students will place icons very sparingly and others will scatter them every few lines. That's not necessarily a problem.

Call time after a few minutes and send kids off to their groups for a short discussion, using the coded sections of the text as conversation starters (e.g., "I was really puzzled here on the bottom of page 23 where Romeo says, 'What light from yonder window breaks?' How can light break?"). As always, we want to make sure the response-harvesting tool we have just taught is actually feeding strong, self-sustaining conversations.

Alone

From childhood's hour I have not been

As others were; I have not seen

As others saw; I could not bring

My passions from a common spring. ✓ *Poe was a weird kid*

From the same source I have not taken

My sorrow; I could not awaken

My heart to joy at the same tone; ✓

And all I loved, I loved alone. ✱ *lonely*

Then- in my childhood, in the dawn

Of a most stormy life- was drawn

From every depth of good and ill

The mystery which binds me still: *? ?*

From the torrent, or the fountain,

From the red cliff of the mountain,

From the sun that round me rolled

In its autumn tint of gold,

From the lightning in the sky

As it passed me flying by, *?*

From the thunder and the storm,

And the cloud that took the form

(When the rest of Heaven was blue) *?*

Of a demon in my view. ✱ *cloud looks like a demon to Poe*

– Edgar Allen Poe

Reflecting

When debriefing the coding system, remember to talk about the reading selection first—its content, ideas, and style—before you start reviewing the pros and cons of the new system. When you shift to talking about the tool itself, here's a good way to begin: "How did this work for you, as a reader and as a group member, compared to the other strategies we have learned, like journaling and role sheets?" You can have kids jot in their journals for a couple of minutes first, or just go directly into whole-class conversation.

If you practice text coding last, as we have ordered it here in the book, this is a natural time to talk with students about what tools they plan to use with their future readings. After all these experiments, your students should have some sense of what works best for them and be able to explain how they've come to that conclusion. Perhaps you'll announce at this point that kids can choose their own most comfortable and productive form of harvesting reading responses for future books and discussions.

What Can Go Wrong?

The most predictable problem with text coding, as with many other newly learned strategies, is overuse. Kids may scatter asterisks and question marks all through the text but forget what half of them mean. You may need to help with a limit, such as five marks per page, to make sure the really big ideas get attention. Or, at the bottom of each page, students might write a short response that will help them remember why they coded the text as they did.

Similarly, some kids love highlighters so much that their books end up looking like they were printed on yellow paper, with everything (and consequently nothing) highlighted. This is the latest equivalent of students who underline almost every sentence in the textbook, which only makes the textbook harder to read. So, if you're going to add highlighting to the mix, be ready to add a sub-mini-lesson on determining what's important. You can easily do this with another short text selection: Have kids mark the three most important sections or ideas and then briefly discuss those items.

Chances are the conversation will be much more focused than if you had let kids overdo their highlighting.

Finally, if students want to code materials they are not allowed to mark up (like textbooks or library copies), get a supply of tiny sticky notes (one by two inches) for them to use.

chapter

4

Getting Started with Whole Books

By now, you have built a foundation of collaborative social skills by nurturing a high level of friendship, open communication, and productive work habits. This doesn't mean you've got a classroom full of angels or 100 percent on-task behavior, 24–7. But you do have a positive climate, and the kids know what social skills they are supposed to demonstrate. They've also been practicing the cognitive strategies needed to find worthy discussion topics while reading. You've showed them several tools they can use to record those connections, questions, feelings, and critiques and present them in a small-group conversation.

Up to this point, you've probably been using short texts—news articles, poems, short stories—as practice material. Now it's time to move up to whole books.

The first time kids work in full-fledged literature circles, there are quite a few procedures to address: selecting books, forming groups, making a workable schedule, and learning to read and talk as a group. In this chapter, we provide mini-lessons for each of these key steps, including two different ways to help each kid find a just-right book, since this choice is so crucial to the success of book clubs. Because literature circles stress student responsibility, the kids, not you, should be taking on these tasks. You'll retain some control over group formation to ensure that you have wholesome, smooth-functioning groups, especially for this first round of whole books. But the rest is up to the kids, as facilitated by the following lessons.

First, though, a note about the books themselves. We want to offer students as wide a choice as we can. Just as adult reading groups select from a universe of titles, we want students to enjoy a range of genres, authors, topics, and levels of difficulty. This means you need a good collection of books, in sets of four to six copies each, in your classroom. Most teachers are pretty familiar with begging, borrowing, and stealing to build such a collection and understand that it is a career-long process. But if your collection is small, or limited to class sets, you can certainly do a whole-class book in literature-circle style. In fact, some of our colleagues intentionally have their kids read the same book for the first cycle of lit circles, so that everyone can compare notes—not just on the process of becoming effective book clubs, but also on the story content. But ultimately, the great thing about true literature circles where each group has picked a different title, is that all students will be reading books they really like, every time. If we teachers always pick the books, aiming for some mythical "middle of the class" or to meet a state mandate, that simply will not happen. Maybe we need to occasionally recite this mantra: Choice is at the core of lifelong reading.

Once your students have completed their first cycle of book clubs, you shouldn't need to repeat all the following steps when they pick their next set of books. However, if you "mothball" literature circles for weeks or months, devoting the time to other curriculum demands, expect amnesia to set in, and plan to redo some or all of these lessons.

Presenting Book Choices with Book Talks

Why Do It?

Literature circles permit truly differentiated instruction in the classroom. Within one set of choices, books can range from easy reads to highly mature titles—something for everyone. However, for the groups to be successful and enjoy their reading, members have to make truly informed choices. One way to accomplish this is to have students rank their interest in the possible titles as you describe each one.

Teaching the Lesson

Getting Started

Ahead of time, gather sample copies of the literature circle choices, copy ballots that list the titles (see the sample ballot for the Revolutionary War), and instruct the students to rank their choices one through three *after* all of the books have been described. When previewing the books, highlight the plots and give students information that might help them make suitable choices. For example, in Nancy's American Studies class, one of the book choices for the unit on World War II was *The Eye of the Needle* by Ken Follett. Here's her book talk.

The Eye of the Needle is a riveting suspense novel about a German spy and professional assassin who uncovers information that could very well derail the invasion of Normandy if he is successful in transmitting his information back to Hitler in time. Whenever anyone interferes with his mission or recognizes his real identity, Faber, nicknamed "Die Nadel," which is German for The Needle, coldly kills with his stiletto knife.

In the beginning, this book jumps around quite a bit between characters and locations, but if you know that ahead of time you won't get confused. Also, since this book was written for adults, there are some scenes of violence as well as sexual intimacy. If anyone finds that offensive, then don't pick it!

As it turned out, two groups of boys ended up reading this book. They had great discussions about World War II and the role spies played for both the Allied and Axis nations. Ironically, they found the "adult scenes" rather tame. Cable and satellite TV have made their mark. The key to good book talks is keeping each summary brief while including some high-interest details that will hook the kids.

After we've completed the book talks, students review their ballots and rank their choices. As we collect the ballots, we warn the kids that, while we'll try to give them their first choice, we can only guarantee that everyone will get one of his or her top three choices. Then, after class, we sort the ballots by first choice. Lots of times a couple of books will prove enormously popular, but most classrooms have a finite number of each title, so often a second sorting is necessary. This time we take a closer look at who chose what. Our aim is always to form groups of four or five individuals who will get along and want to read the book. At this point ballots are shifted according to those criteria, and the final groups are chosen.

Working the Room

Because students fill out their ballots individually, little monitoring takes place other than keeping students quiet. Sometimes they want to shout across the room to their friends in order to pick the same book. We

Sample Ballot

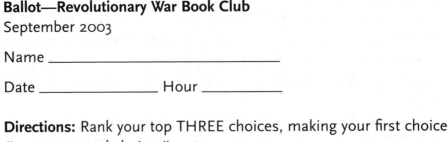

Ballot—Revolutionary War Book Club

September 2003

Name _____

Date _____ Hour _____

Directions: Rank your top THREE choices, making your first choice #1, your second choice #2, etc.

_____ *The Fifth of March*

_____ *Fever 1793*

_____ *Rise to Rebellion*

_____ *Redcoat*

_____ *The Bastard*

_____ *The Rebels*

_____ *Johnny Tremain*

_____ *Cast Two Shadows*

_____ *My Brother Sam Is Dead*

---

discourage this since we'd rather have students base their selections on what interests them versus what their friends want them to read just to keep long-running posses together.

Reflecting

When the chosen literature circle books are first passed out, we like to have the kids read for about twenty minutes and then write dialogue journals (see pages 63–70) with a partner who is reading the same book. We ask them to write about what they remember about the initial book talk, why they ranked that book highly on the ballot, and what they've noticed after reading the first chapter or so. After finishing the book, it's interesting for the students to revisit that initial piece of writing and see how their initial expectations matched what the book had to offer.

What Can Go Wrong?

Sometimes students choose books that just don't seem to fit them at all, at least from your perspective. That's when you need to pull the student aside and confer privately. Often the kids will surprise you with specific reasons for the choice and prove that they know more about themselves as readers than you do. Other times the student may have gotten the titles confused and really meant to pick a different one. We've also found it valuable to emphasize how long a book is. Nancy makes it a point to turn longer books sideways and say, "See how thick this book is? It's a great book, but it's thick. I just want you to remember that." Otherwise, we've found that one or two kids will always be shocked when they get a long book, the one they marked #1 on the ballot. On the other hand, making kids well aware of a book's length doesn't seem to discourage too many of them from picking it up. Nancy has had no problem getting kids to choose books 800 pages long. As long as they enter the agreement with full knowledge, it's not a problem, and they'll finish the book at the same time as the group who chose the 150-page tome.

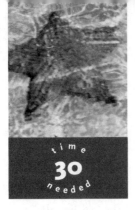

Presenting Book Choices with a Book Pass

Why Do It?

For literature circles to really soar, every student must be reading a book that is thoroughly engrossing and just right for them. But sometimes, even when you give them a few days to browse all the possible selections for the next round of book clubs, not all students do so. And even your most dynamic book talks don't earn rapt attention when you are blurbing six or eight titles, one after another. Doing a "book pass" takes a little more time but guarantees that every kid will sample each possible choice and make a truly informed selection.

The process is nothing complicated. It's just a structured way for kids to read two minutes' worth of every available book choice. When we use this activity, we often see kids choosing books they would not otherwise have read, stretching themselves into new genres and authors, and sometimes hooking up with new combinations of peers.

Teaching the Lesson

Getting Started

Set up "stations" (tables if you have them; pushed-together desks, if not) with four seats each. At each station, place one copy of four different titles that kids can select for their next book club cycle. (Depending on the number of kids and choices, you might need to have three books and three kids, or five books and five kids—just so the math comes out right.) Hand out sheets like the Book Pass Review Sheet provided in the appendix, or have students make notes in their journals. Then explain how the book pass will work:

When you sit down at a table, grab a book. Don't fight over them—everybody is going to sample each one. When I say "go," start at page 1, Chapter 1, and read as far as you can until I call "stop" in two minutes. Keep reading as fast as you can. When you stop, I'll give you thirty seconds to fill out the review sheets, so you'll remember which books you liked and why. Then pass your book to the left and repeat; read, write, and pass until you've sampled all four books. I'll be calling out the times to keep you on schedule.

If there are only three to five choices in all, one sitting does the job. If you're able to offer kids a broader choice (six to eight titles or more), then the fun really begins. After "tasting" all the books at one table, kids move to the next station, where you have placed four different books, and the cycle repeats. Some of our veteran lit circle teachers have big classroom libraries of multiple-copy sets. In their rooms, a book pass can have four different books at three or four tables, representing twelve to sixteen choices! (Working through this many choices takes longer, of course, and stays fresher if done at two sittings.)

Working the Room

Your main job is to call out the two-minute intervals, keep your eye on the tables, and usher kids along. When students have sampled and rated all of the possible titles, have them write you a note listing their top three choices in order of preference. Then collect these ballots and, at your leisure, form groups built around kids' interests, factoring in your appraisal of their reading level and the need to make smooth-running, productive groups. If you think a student has picked a book that's too hard, use a private conference, note, or email to review the decision. If you and the student agree that the book is just too tough, suggest an alternative from the other choices. But also be open-minded; if a struggling reader is really fascinated with the topic, is willing to make the effort necessary to get through the book, and will be in a supportive group of peers, let him take the risk, and provide backup (such as books on tape) where you can.

....

Reflecting

Have kids talk about what books (or, rather, book openings) they liked and why. Happily, for once, everyone will have actually read the text being discussed! Be careful to collect the kids' ballots first, before the discussion reveals that their usual posse has selected another book or someone has trashed their number-one choice.

In a more literary vein, this is an ideal time to talk about how authors start a book, how they get us hooked. The eminent literary scholar Alfred Appel says that a great writer will tell you the whole story of the book in the first paragraph if you know how to listen. If Appel is right, kids should be able to predict much about the book just from reading the first few pages.

What Can Go Wrong?

This activity is so brisk that it rarely goes astray. The most common problem with book passes, a rather delicious one, is that sometimes a student will get so hooked on a book that she won't pass it along after the allotted two minutes. We've even had kids refuse to leave the table when it's time to move to the next station and try the next four books. While we do love it when kids make this sudden connection with a book, it sure can clog the smooth flow of a book pass. The crude solution to this problem is to pry the book from the offending reader's hand and forcibly pass it along. But why come between a reader and a new love? If we are really growing lifelong readers with our literature circles, we want to nurture, not quash, that magical head-over-heels experience with a book. The simple answer: Have a few extra copies of each book so you can replenish the table and avoid a logjam, and let the smitten student read on.

A rare but annoying problem is when kids who have already read one of the books either trash-talk it or give away the ending. If lots of kids have read a book choice before, you may need to warn against these sins at the outset.

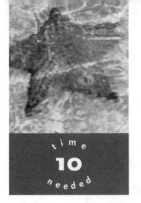

time
10
needed

Setting Ground Rules

Why Do It?

Even though we teachers have a pretty clear idea of what literature circle meetings should look like, it's much better for students to develop their own expectations and set their own standards. These expectations come under the heading of Ground Rules.

Teaching the Lesson

Getting Started

After students have gathered in their new literature circle groups, introduced each other, and completed discussion of a Membership Grid topic, it's time to develop their Ground Rules. We say:

> *Think about the past groups you've been in, both in and out of this class. What kinds of behaviors helped groups succeed? What kind of behaviors made meetings a chore or unproductive? In order for your group to work well together, come up with three to five common expectations or Ground Rules that everyone agrees to abide by. We'll compare notes in seven minutes.*

At this point the groups commence their individual discussions, decide which rules are most important for success, and write them down in their journals.

Student Ground Rule Examples

Group #1

1) Come prepared and ready
2) Listen to what others have to say
3) Stay on task
4) Make eye contact
5) Ask follow-up questions

Group #2

1) Read pages by the due date
2) Come prepared with passages, questions, and pictures
3) Have confidence in members and their ideas
4) Address others by name
5) Have fun

After they're finished, have a spokesperson from each group read their Ground Rules to the rest of the class; this helps everyone see that expectations for successful interaction do not vary that much from group to group. Sometimes a group comes up with a rule no one else thought of, yet seems like a pretty good idea. Hearing the other lists can help a group realize they missed something important that needs to be stated clearly in their own rules. After the large-group share, have students huddle for five minutes in their small groups to review and revise their Ground Rules.

Working the Room

As you visit each group, have one member read the new Ground Rules aloud to you. If they're missing something you consider major, here's your chance to jump in with "Have you considered . . . ?" But once you've inserted your two cents, walk away! The point is for the group members to take responsibility for their decisions.

Reflecting

When groups have completed their final rule revisions, have students reflect on them individually in their journals. We like to ask three questions:

- Which rule will be the easiest for you to follow?

- Which rule is going to give you the most difficulty?

- What plans can you make now that will decrease the likelihood of your letting your group down?

What Can Go Wrong?

Two problems can arise with the Ground Rules. The first is that the kids might not take the assignment seriously and will come up with some weird rules. However, vigilant monitoring combined with the question, "How will this rule help your group to be successful?" is usually enough to turn a group around.

The second problem is that, like any rules, these require review and reflection. Just like the U.S. Constitution, a group's Ground Rules is a living document. "Articles" can be amended or changed when necessary. Also, groups need to discuss how well they are living up to their own expectations and actively use the Ground Rules to help improve future discussions, so it's a good idea to have literature circles review their Ground Rules at the beginning or end of every discussion.

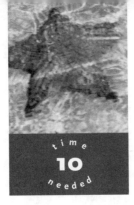

time
10
needed

Making a Reading Calendar

Why Do It?

Part of the charm of literature circles is that kids take a lot of responsibility for their learning and behavior. Though the teacher usually decides on the literature circle meeting dates and the date the book must be finished, each student group decides how much reading is due for each meeting.

Teaching the Lesson

Getting Started

Before the first meeting, create a calendar and make copies for each student, plus at least one extra for each group. Before duplicating the calendars, be sure to note major holidays or other school events (homecoming, prom, etc.) that might affect reading assignments. Also, mark the dates for the literature circle meetings. Scheduling the meetings on the same day(s) of the week adds a sense of predictability that can be useful.

Pass out the calendars before the kids move into their groups. Using an overhead transparency of the calendar, explain: "In a moment your groups will get together and negotiate the reading assignments." Point out the meeting dates and any dates that might affect their ability to do homework. For example, having the biggest chunk of reading due the Monday after homecoming is never a good idea. Also, instruct the kids that they need to list the actual start and stop pages for each assignment rather than just the chapter numbers.

Sample Reading Calendar

GROUP #1   The Great Escape

April 2003 / May

Sun	Mon	Tue	Wed	Thu	Fri	Sat
13	14	15	16	(17) p1–60 **Book Club Meeting #1**	18 Good Friday No School	19
20	21	22	23 State Exams	24 State Exams	(25) p60–120 **Book Club Meeting #2**	26
27	28 **History Article #1 Due**	29	30	1 **May**	(2) p120–180 **Book Club Meeting #3**	3
4	5 **History Article #2 Due**	6	7	8	(9) p180–236 **Book Club Meeting #4**	10
11	12	13	14 **Book Club Essays Due**	15 Performance Projects	16 Institute Day Jr/Sr Prom	17

Students then move into their groups and figure out their reading schedules. If more than one group is reading the same book, particularly if some groups have only three members, it's a good idea for those groups to meet together and develop a mutual calendar. That way if one of the groups experiences severe attrition due to absences, they can easily combine with the other group and not miss a beat.

Once groups have determined their calendars, give them an extra copy and tell them to copy the information for you. You'll be able to keep much better track of every group's reading if you have a copy of their calendars.

Working the Room

Make sure that students are writing down page numbers rather than chapter numbers. Encourage them to do the math and figure out exactly how many pages they plan to read for each meeting. However, watch out for the group that takes the math angle to the extreme. Rather than eyeballing the chapters for logical breaks, this group will divide the total number of pages by the number of meetings; consequently their reading assignments can end in the most unlikely spots, like one paragraph before the big climax. As you monitor, ask the groups to explain the logic behind their reading schedules.

Reflecting

After the first meeting or two, groups should review their calendars and see if they need to make any changes. Some groups will realize that they've completely miscalculated their assignments and need to revise them, particularly if this is their first stab at developing a calendar. Plus, students will develop a good sense of their own reading speed and pages-per-day capacity within certain genres of text, which can serve them well with later book choices.

What Can Go Wrong?

The only problem with the calendar is that it doesn't guarantee that students will complete the assigned reading. Dealing with unprepared students is covered in Chapter 6.

Variation

Negotiated calendars can be used for any project that has a series of steps. Consider the process of writing a research paper. Rather than assigning the due dates for each piece of the process, explain what each step entails. Then give the kids a list of the steps and a calendar marked with the day the papers are due, along with any other dates etched in stone (such as your class's reservations for the computer lab). Using pencils, each group figures out a tentative schedule. The final step is to work out the schedule as a class or send one representative from each group into the hall to develop the final schedule, which will be duplicated for everyone.

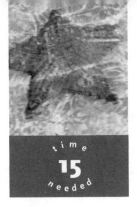

Dealing with the
First Chapter

Why Do It?

Sometimes it's hard for students to get started on a new book, particularly if the text is challenging. Instead of having kids struggle on their own to prepare adequate notes for the first literature circle session, it's often helpful to let groups have a less formal first-chapter meeting.

Teaching the Lesson

Getting Started

After the literature circle groups have created their Ground Rules and calendars, have the members take a few silent minutes to peruse their new books, examining the title, cover art, cover or inside blurbs, table of contents, and so forth. Then have students set up a two-column chart in their journals and write down three predictions in the first column. In the second column, they note their reasons for their predictions. To discourage kids from simply copying directly from the cover, we might say: "When you look at the cover, use your imagination. We want you to look carefully at the cover art and plot information, but predict some story details that aren't specifically mentioned. Your prediction should bring up something new yet plausible."

After all members in the group have made their individual predictions, have them share their ideas, mainly looking to see how students thought alike and where they diverged in their thinking.

Mike's Initial Predictions for *Dances with Wolves*

Prediction	Reasons
The main character will be John Dunbar and he is going to have to make a major decision about what he believes in. Dunbar will be a rugged, tough guy.	Big picture of a man the front cover along w..., the phrase "battle with himself was just the beginning." Back cover mentions name. Guy in photo looks rugged.
Dunbar is lonely and longs for something; maybe he'll get married, have kids.	Cover says Civil War is over. Back cover mentions abandoned army post, loneliness, Comanches keeping him company.
Dunbar gives up being a soldier. Becomes a Comanche, but someone finds out and tries to have him arrested as a traitor.	Back cover describes Dunbar as becoming more Indian but then his past comes back to haunt him.

Either in class after the quick prediction meeting or for homework that night, students read the first chapter, using sticky notes to mark

- the introduction of new characters
- setting details
- places where they were confused

The following day, the groups meet to make sure everyone is on the right track. They need to trade information on characters and setting and clear up the points members found confusing. Also, if the book has a "cast of thousands," it's a good idea for students to keep a running "who's who" list in their journals or on a bookmark so that they can keep track of the characters.

Working the Room

Be sure that everyone in the group has written some predictions before they begin talking. Also, watch that members don't just read their predictions and stop; they need to also explain what led to their ideas. Kids will sometimes define "predicting" as making up whatever they want. You can't start too early requiring them to anchor their ideas to specific sections of the book.

Reflecting

After students have discussed their initial predictions and the first chapter, have them discuss the following questions and then record the group's ideas in their journals. Toward the end of the book, members can return to this entry and compare their early thinking to later conclusions drawn from further reading:

- How did your predictions based on the book cover change after reading the first chapter?
- Which first-chapter predictions does everyone seem to agree on?
- Which characters has your group decided will be the most important ones? Why?

What Can Go Wrong?

As students work on their initial predictions, look over their shoulders and read what they've written. Remind students that predictions do need to relate to the known text in some way; forecasts that include the intervention of Martians or The Terminator do not count. Also, if a prediction is taken verbatim from the information on the back cover, then it's not really a prediction—the answer has already been revealed.

Variations

In addition to discussions of initial predictions, dialogue journals are another effective way for students to start a discussion after reading the first chapter (see Chapter 2). Also, predictions can be used again when students are about one-third of the way through their books. At that point, we like to use the lesson called The Envelope, Please in Chapter 7.

Making initial predictions and posing questions comes in handy when studying current events. If you want students to follow a news story as it unfolds, have them read the initial story and then write predictions and questions. Then send them off to follow the story in the newspaper or on the Internet.

5

Refining Discussion Skills: Creating Deeper Comprehension

The quality and depth of student book club meetings is high on a teacher's list of concerns. When kids digress from the text, get stuck on superficial plot details, skip over important elements, or act rudely toward each other, we all get nervous. After all the work we have done to set up literature circles—choosing books, forming groups, creating schedules, and beginning the reading—we want to be sure that ensuing discussions are of high quality: thoughtful, sustained, and genuinely collaborative.

As we admitted earlier, the initial training we provided, however careful, is never enough. To further support kids' conversation development, we might start the next few meetings with mini-lessons aimed at sharpening a key discussion skill, such as

- asking good questions

- asking follow-up questions

- getting everyone involved

- grounding arguments in the book

- practicing individual discussion skills

- using notes more effectively to feed discussions

Each of the mini-lessons in this chapter isolates and strengthens one of these small-group skills.

The first two skills are especially critical because they directly address the way we want students to talk to each other. They show that open-ended, well-chosen questions can drive the conversations in book clubs, just as they do in life. Indeed, the quality and quantity of questions that members have for each other determines, to a great extent, the success of any discussion group. Therefore, we tend to do these two mini-lessons with almost every class. The other four address somewhat narrower discussion skills, and you would choose among them by noticing what your group needs next. As always, you monitor the skill as kids put it to work in class, and then debrief it at the end of the meetings.

Asking Good Questions

time
20
needed

Why Do It?

Students often have difficulty coming up with good questions for discussion. Considering that most kids have experienced only rapid-fire large-group discussions, this is not surprising. The typical whole-class discussion question is based on a short-answer response. Questions that require extended and complicated answers seldom work because answering them requires individual kids to take a greater risk. And even if a brave student speaks up, an extended focus on one person often loses the attention of the rest of the class. Since most students have experienced few models of the kind of questioning that works best for small-group discussion, directly addressing this skill is vital.

Teaching the Lesson

Getting Started

After the second or third literature circle discussion, have students fold a page in their journals lengthwise to create two columns. They then label the left-hand column "Good Questions" and the right-hand column "Characteristics." Next, students review their discussion notes and jot down six questions: three that created an interesting and extended conversation and—under the label "Bad Questions"—three that didn't work very well.

After completing this first step, students examine their questions with a partner and try to figure out why some worked while others did not. The next figure shows one student's chart for *Middle Passage.*

Good Questions

Why did Rutherford leave Southern Illinois?

Why did he take the log book?

Why did Falcon crumple up Rutherford's papers?

Characteristics

More than one answer may be right.

Leads to theories and what you think will happen.

Makes you talk about other things that happened in the book.

No one's opinion is wrong so no one gets made fun of.

Bad Questions

Why would she force Rutherford to marry her?

Why would Rutherford need a pistol?

Why does Falcon have all his stuff rigged?

Some of those questions get answered in like the next paragraph.

Questions just require short answers, not much to discuss.

Require no opinions or details.

There's only one right answer.

Finally, with the large group, make a master list of what makes a question good or bad.

Conclude the activity by having students return to their original questions and decide what characteristics from the master list their questions reflected. Then have students set a couple of new question goals for their next discussion. Many times students fall into a rut, asking the same types of

Question Characteristics

Good Questions

- Are not easily answered—make you think.
- Have more than one possible answer.
- Lead to different opinions/ viewpoints.
- Make people interpret why something happens or a character does something.
- Make you predict the ending or future problems.
- Pose comparisons.
- Get you emotionally involved.
- Make you fill in details from your imagination.
- Bring up controversial ideas.
- Make you notice something you didn't before.
- Make you see something in a different way.
- Help you understand the book better.
- Pull different parts of the book together.
- Make you put yourself in the characters' shoes.
- Lead to more follow-up questions.
- Connect the book with personal experiences.
- Focus on important parts of the story.
- Are interesting and get attention.

Bad Questions

- Have a yes or no answer.
- You can easily find the answer.
- Ask for one specific detail—not much to talk about.
- Nothing to disagree or argue about.
- Only one opinion is possible.
- Ask about something that isn't important to the story.
- Don't help people understand the book better.
- Make it hard to think of follow-up questions.
- Don't make you go back to the book.
- Have obvious answers; don't take much thinking.
- Don't connect with other parts of story.
- Don't make members solve a problem or use imagination.
- Have nothing to do with the book.
- Are too vague, too general.

questions over and over. Their goal is to write different kinds of questions that will elicit different yet lively responses from their groups.

Working the Room

The time to cruise the room during this strategy is when the kids are working with their partners. Make sure they understand that everyone should be prepared because all pairs will be expected to contribute.

Reflecting

After the next discussion, students revisit the goals that were set during the previous good-question mini-lesson and see how they did. Which questions created the best discussion this time? How did they make that happen?

What Can Go Wrong?

If students are still having trouble writing good questions, they probably need more direct coaching. Take a break from the literature circles and read three short stories as a class. After reading the first story silently, have students brainstorm some good questions with a partner, using the good question characteristics list developed earlier. Then share the questions in the whole group, with partners explaining why their question is a good one.

After reading the second story silently, have partners once again brainstorm good questions together. Next, have students find new partners and instruct them to take turns asking each other the questions as they continue the discussion. End by sharing some of the questions with the whole class and discussing what made them good.

For the last story, have students read and work on their own to create some good questions. Then have them return to their literature circles, aiming for an interesting discussion that examines the story in some depth and uses follow-up questions. As in the previous examples, end by sharing some of the best questions the groups discussed.

After this question study, students should definitely know what constitutes a good question. If you notice that a few students continue to pose poor questions, take them aside for some private coaching/cajoling. At this point, those students know what good questions are but don't want to take the time or effort to come up with them. After all, it does take more thought to develop a good question than one whose answer can be found on the next page!

Variation

Developing good questions is the most important skill when beginning to work on a research paper. Being able to review how interesting questions are made will come in handy for this kind of writing.

Asking Follow-up Questions

Why Do It?

Coming up with good questions to start a conversation is important, but doesn't guarantee that a group will pursue a topic in depth. For extended discussion to occur, the groups need to know how to listen to members' comments carefully and ask open-ended follow-up questions that will get people to explain their ideas in greater detail. This lesson helps students understand what follow-up questions are and improves their performance in using them. We recommend you use this lesson several times during a literature circle cycle since learning how to ask good follow-up questions is probably one of the most difficult—and most fundamental—discussion skills students need to master. This lesson takes some time, so it is a great one to teach between book club meetings.

Teaching the Lesson

....

Getting Started

Model these steps as you describe how to set up the chart:

> *Fold a sheet of loose-leaf paper in half lengthwise to make two columns. Keeping this fold, take the bottom edge and fold it up one third; take the new bottom edge and fold it up one third again. When you open the paper back up, you should have two columns, each*

subdivided into three cells. Label the left-hand column "Starter Question" and the right-hand column "Follow-up Questions."

Pass out a short story and instruct the students to read it carefully and come up with three good starter questions that they think would work well in a group discussion. This is a good time for students to briefly review the list of good-question characteristics that should be in their journals. Each starter question should be recorded in the left-hand column in a separate cell.

For the next step, each student works with a partner. One partner begins by reading his starter question aloud to his partner. The partner listens carefully to the question and then answers. The person who asked the question must ask another question based on something that was in the partner's answer. After asking the second question, the questioner writes the follow-up question in the right-hand column across from the starter question that it corresponds to. The partner who has been answering cannot answer the follow-up question until it is written down. Instead, she must think about the answer she is going to give. Once again, the questioning partner listens carefully and then must come up with another follow-up question. This process is repeated until three follow-up questions have been asked. Then it is the other person's turn to ask the questions and write them down.

The following excerpt is from the beginning of a short speech by Pat Conroy, author of *The Prince of Tides,* featured in *3 Minutes or Less: Life Lessons from America's Greatest Writers* (PEN/Faulkner 2000). We often use this text to train students on lead and follow-up questions. Describing his father's abusive behavior toward his family, this is the way the speech begins:

> My father, a Marine Corps fighter pilot, 200 pounds, six-two, a blunt instrument: a semiautomatic assault weapon. My father waged war against the Japanese, the North Koreans, the Vietnamese, and his family. My first memory: my mother trying to stab my father with a butcher-knife while he was beating her. I knew this was going to be a long and involved life. . . .
>
> The worst thing that happened: Dad was stationed at the Pentagon and a fight broke out between my mother and father when my sister had her birthday party, her ninth birthday party. I was eleven. A fight started. My role was to get the other six kids out of harm's

Lead Question	Follow-up Question
Why would the author remember this of all things?	Do you think the father was drunk? Explain. Do you think the author was ever beaten by his father? Explain. What would happen if someone got killed?
Why would the kid try to get in between his mom, who is trying to stab the dad in defence, and the dad, who is trying to beat his mom?	What do you think gave the author the courage? Why didn't the mother divorce him after this? Why didn't she press charges?

way. So I rushed them out of the room. My second job was to get Mom away from Dad. I went roaring in. I was eleven. Dad could eat Ollie North for breakfast. I get between them. I looked over my head and saw the butcher knife I'd seen when I was a child. My mother connected this time. Blood got on me, my sister. Mother took us to Hot Shoppes and said she was going to leave Dad. She did not.

Working the Room

First, make sure that students wait for the questioner to write the follow-up question down before answering. Emphasize that most of the time in a discussion, people answer too quickly; if they stopped to think for a few seconds, their answers would be more thorough and clear. Second, watch for students who are asking yes or no questions. Point these out and help those students rephrase them as open-ended questions. Finally, be on the lookout for partners who keep asking questions. Once they've moved through one starter question and the three follow-ups, they need to switch. Otherwise, one person will get a lot of questioning practice while the partner gets very little. Also, by the time one person asks all his questions, it often leaves the partner with few new ideas.

Reflections

After students have practiced, ask them to look back at the starter questions and find the one that seemed best at generating follow-up questions. Then have them figure out why this was the case. Realizing how the starter question ties directly into good follow-ups is important. It is also a good idea to have students reflect on how easy or difficult it was for them to think of good follow-ups. Asking follow-ups requires focus, good listening, and quick thinking. All of these take practice.

What Can Go Wrong?

Be sure to model this activity with a partner before you set the class loose in pairs; otherwise, kids may be very confused. Including the modeling, this activity takes about thirty minutes; that's why we suggest that it be used on a book club off-day.

Expect that students will complain that this activity is unnatural and cumbersome. They're right; it is. However, almost any complicated activity must be broken down into simpler components before it is mastered. Have you ever taken golf lessons to improve your swing? Do surgeons immediately begin practicing on live patients because working on cadavers just isn't realistic? Shrug off their complaints and tell the kids that as soon as you see them acing follow-up questions in their literature circle discussions, you won't require any more artificial practice sessions.

What's Next?

As we mentioned earlier, this mini-lesson will probably need to be repeated two or three times before the kids start to internalize the idea that any answer should always have a follow-up question chasing after it.

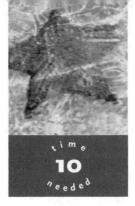

Save the Last Word for Me

Why Do It?

In preparation for literature circle discussions, we often ask kids to pick important passages to bring to the group. Amazingly, students reliably demonstrate their ability to pick great parts. As a matter of fact, lots of times they'll pick the same passages that we would. Unfortunately, even with a wealth of material to work with, their passage discussions often follow this predictable format:

1. Member reads passage aloud.

2. Same member explains why she picked that passage.

3. The rest of group nods in agreement and it's on to the next passage.

Of course, the truly engaging moments in any discussion occur when someone in the group notices text in a different way and then explains a view that no one else had even thought of.

The strategy Save the Last Word for Me (Short, Harste, and Burke 1995) encourages kids to gather ideas from all group members before the person who chose the passage explains his or her interpretations. A good way to introduce this strategy is to say:

Observing your groups the other day, I noticed that the person who reads a passage immediately explains it without encouraging others to share first. Getting more ideas out on the floor is a way to make discussion more interesting, and using Save the Last Word for Me is a way to accomplish this.

138 ■ CHAPTER 5 REFINING DISCUSSION SKILLS

Teaching the Lesson

Getting Started

Choose two passages of text that do not require extensive introductions before they are read aloud. Good choices include short newspaper articles or the opening paragraphs of novels. Make sure students have copies so that they can read along. Model the first passage the way the kids do: Read it aloud and then immediately explain in detail why you chose it. The following passage is from the first two paragraphs of *To Kill a Mockingbird* by Harper Lee.

> When he was nearly thirteen, my brother Jem got his arm badly broken at the elbow. When it healed, and Jem's fears of never being able to play football were assuaged, he was seldom self-conscious about his injury. . . .
>
> When enough years had gone by to enable us to look back on them, we sometimes discussed the events leading to his accident. I maintain that the Ewells started it all, but Jem, who was four years my senior, said it started long before that. He said it began the summer Dill came to us, when Dill first gave us the idea of making Boo Radley come out.

Teacher's Explanation: *I chose this passage because it makes me ask a lot of questions. How did Jem's arm get broken? Why are they still talking about it years later? What does Jem's arm have to do with Boo Radley? What does it mean that Dill made him come out? Why was he hiding? Why did they even care about him? Who are the Ewells? It sounds like the narrator blames them for Jem's broken arm. Considering that Jem's big concern was playing football, it seems like it's the narrator who can't stop thinking about this incident rather than Jem. He seems okay with it. That word "assuaged" is interesting. I wonder what it means.*

Then you might say, "Okay, that's what I think. Let's get some ideas from some other readers," and call on a few kids at random. After that passage explanation, you can bet there won't be any other ideas because the kids already heard an extended version of "the right" answer. Their thinking has been shut down. When this happens, mention that you've noticed the same thing happening during their literature circle meetings.

Before reading the second passage aloud, have students review the reading/thinking strategies that they brainstormed during the Think-Aloud modeling done earlier. Now say, "As I read this second passage aloud, I want you to follow along and notice what the passage makes you think about. After hearing the passage, everyone should be ready to have something to say about it."

After reading the second passage, explain the new strategy: "Now we're going to Save the Last Word for Me. Before I say anything about this passage, I want to hear what some of you have to say. Tell the rest of us why you think the passage was important, how that passage relates to something else in the story, or just what you noticed and thought about as that passage was read." Then call on three or four kids at random before you explain why you chose it.

Students should notice that it's easier to think of a response before the reader explains anything and that their ideas are often different from the reader's.

Now the groups have their marching orders. Whenever someone reads a passage aloud, the only thing the reader can say at first is "Save the Last Word for Me." Not until everyone else has contributed an opinion can the person who chose the passage explain his thoughts.

Working the Room

Though this strategy seems deceptively simple, it is not. Primed by reading the passage aloud, many students immediately want to share their thoughts. As you observe the literature circles in action, you'll need to gently prod and remind the kids to "Save the Last Word" because it's guaranteed that some will forget.

Reflecting

A good way for students to reflect on what they talked about is to have them pick out the most interesting passage of the day and then jot down the different ideas that came out of its discussion. Also, if you notice that most of the groups are forgetting to Save the Last Word, the members need to develop a specific plan for improving the use of this strategy. Here are some ideas former students have suggested:

- Assign one person to enforce the Save the Last Word rule.

- Write STLW (Save the Last Word) in big letters on each sticky note that marks a passage.

- Make Save the Last Word bookmarks as a reminder.

- Turn Save the Last Word into a friendly competition. Once a passage is read, members try to see who can blurt out "Save the Last Word for Me!" first.

What Can Go Wrong?

Groups can fall into a predictable response pattern when using Save the Last Word. Someone reads a passage, and Chatty Cathy always takes the first swing. By the time it's Silent Sam's turn at the plate, all of the good ideas have been hit out of the park, and he ends up just repeating Cathy's ideas or agreeing with what was already said. When this problem arises, you'll need to directly intervene because a group seldom fixes this problem on its own. Why? Because the group likes the arrangement! The members who have lots to say get to say it, and the ones who are quiet get to comfortably fade away. However, the person who talks the most about a subject usually learns the most as well, so it's important that groups recognize the need to let their quieter members take their best shots first. Besides, even after Silent Sam has his say, Chatty Cathy will have plenty of ideas left to keep the conversation rolling!

Variations

Save the Last Word is also an excellent strategy to use with student drawings, one of the response tools discussed in Chapter 3. Before the artist can explain anything about her picture, everyone else has to speculate about it. Students should be encouraged to focus on not just what is in the picture, but also what happened in the story before and after that scene, as well as what else was going on but was not directly described in the text.

time
20
needed

Prove It! Taking It
Back to the Book

Why Do It?

Teachers often worry that peer-led book club meetings will stray too far from the literature, that kids will spend whole class periods talking about the latest video game, the geeky new kid in school, or the upcoming dance—anything and everything but the book in front of them. That's a legitimate concern. We're willing to let kids orbit around a book, but we do want to keep them somewhere inside the gravitational field (within a few million miles) of the actual story.

But before we implement tough structures to enforce on-task behavior and on-point conversation, let's remember what really happens in adult book clubs, the kind that meet in living rooms, church basements, and community centers around the country. If you observe these groups, you'll find that participants frequently veer off onto wide tangents, long digressions, and idiosyncratic personal connections, without penalty. If you're there from the start, you can track how the book sparked these seemingly distant topics, but someone coming in mid-meeting might ask, "What the hell does *this* have to do with the book?" The point is that real-life book clubs, which are gatherings of the kinds of lifelong readers we want our students to become, tolerate (even welcome) pretty free-ranging conversations. Of course, when we transplant book clubs into the school setting, the rules may have to be adjusted a bit, but just how much?

In addition to off-task behavior, teachers worry about kids coming up with odd, dubious, or just plain wrong interpretations of a book, and not being challenged by their peers. Even Bob Probst, the guru of reader response theory, reminds us that while we respect individual responses to literature, we have a teacherly right—even an obligation—to challenge kids' thinking, to gently defend the idea of better and worse readings of a text.

We think the answer to both these worries—unanchored discussion and insupportable interpretations—is "taking it back to the book." This means building a strong "culture of evidence" in classroom book club meetings, where kids know they must back up their inferences, arguments, and interpretations by reference to specific passages in the book.

Prove It starts with having kids mark and/or write notes about important passages, using one of the six tools outlined in Chapter 3. When they come to book club meetings with specific passages flagged, they are much more likely to be able (and willing) to defend an interpretation or point of view. There are many ways to introduce and nurture the "prove it" mindset. The main thing is that students practice, practice, practice anchoring their ideas to the book.

Teaching the Lesson

Getting Started

Hand out copies of a short story, poem, news article, or common fairy tale and ask everyone to read it, employing their usual note-taking strategy. Kids will flag plenty of sections where interpretation and inference are required, where different opinions are possible, or where controversy might even erupt. Then start posing inferential, interpretive questions, one at a time, and invite volunteers to respond aloud. For this demonstration, we often use *The Three Little Pigs.*

- What do you think the pigs' parents were like?
- What kind of relationships do the brother pigs have?
- Was the wolf evil?
- Was the wolf more or less clever than the average wolf?
- How could these three confrontations have been avoided?

- Why don't the pigs know how to avoid wolves?

- What's the moral of the story?

When a student offers an answer, you simply command, "prove it!" and require the student to point out one or more specific passages that support the interpretation. You'll probably have to wait a few seconds, but what you're looking for is a response like this:

Well, it says right here at the bottom of page three that the big brother pig just laughed at the others. I mean, that's cold—what a way to treat your own family. That's why I said the pigs were not real brothers to each other.

Once a view and its anchor in the book have been offered, invite contrary interpretations with their evidence: "Who sees the pigs' family dynamic another way? What makes you say that?"

After this whole-class demonstration, give students a different short text to work with, something that's open to lots of different views and opinions. Put them to work with this instruction:

Read the piece and mark two places where you have an opinion, interpretation, or idea that can be backed up by specific lines or details in the story. Then meet in your groups and take turns introducing your points and showing the evidence. The other kids in each group, if you see an alternative view that can be supported in the text, bring that up and compare your evidence.

After about five minutes, solicit ideas from the group about how opinions were proven—or not. End by saying, "Remember to take it back to the book in your lit circle discussion. When someone gives an opinion, don't forget to ask them where they got that idea. Don't accept an interpretation without some proof behind it!"

Working the Room

When groups move from the practice piece to the discussion of their books, sit in on each group for two or three minutes. You will be able to tell pretty quickly whether students are successfully tying their discussion to specific parts of the book. If they are, move on. When you land in a struggling group, just wait for the next kid to make an unsupported point and ask:

- Just what in the book makes you say that?
- Can you show us where you got that idea?
- Where's your evidence for that point?

Then be patient as the student flips through the book to locate the spot—or another kid in the group volunteers some evidence. This is good, simple coaching: backing up the mini-lesson with immediate practice and feedback.

Reflecting

After students practice tying ideas directly to the text and you have done some coaching in the groups, you don't need to beat this idea to death in the debriefing. We like to ask kids: What happened when you applied the prove-it rule? Did it change the nature of the discussions? Did you talk about something you might have missed otherwise? Did it lead you to any new ideas? How did it affect the flow of conversation?

What Can Go Wrong?

"Taking it back to the book" is one of those skills, like several we've mentioned earlier, that students may overuse at first. Discussions can slow down and lose their zip if students challenge each other to prove every single comment or assertion. "Prove that her sweater was green!" You may need to use debriefing time (or another mini-lesson) to talk about what kinds of interpretations really need to be proven with text.

Teaching this lesson provides no guarantee that kids will grasp all the themes in a book or will come to the "correct" interpretation every time. It can be agonizing when kids misread a character, skim over the symbolism, or miss the allegory completely. But we have to keep reminding ourselves—these are young readers, starting out on a path that we have been traveling far longer. Forcing our grown-up views on them will not enhance their enjoyment, motivation, or sense of ownership. During other parts of the school schedule, when we are teaching a whole-class book, we can make sure they "get it all." But in book clubs, enjoyment is enough.

Variations

For more Prove-It practice, put kids into their book clubs with another text and a short list of open-ended, interpretive questions. The job is to develop text-supported answers to each item. After five minutes, call the class back and work through the questions, inviting different groups to point out the text that supports a specific answer to the question. Encourage controversy, so that proofs must be thoughtful enough to withstand challenge.

Discussion Skill Table Cards

Why Do It?

We don't want to shock you, but students often forget to use the skills that enhance their literature circle discussions. Even though these important behaviors have been defined via brilliant teacher modeling, T-charts, posters, and processing, students will still forget. That's because using a new skill requires us to reconstruct our patterns of interaction, and it is human nature to unconsciously slip back into our old comfortable habits. One way to take kids to the next level of owning a skill is through the use of table cards (Kagan 1994).

Teaching the Lesson

Getting Started

To introduce this lesson, simply describe what you've been seeing in the groups so far. Most groups are probably on task but may be having somewhat superficial and listless conversations. Emphasize that high-performing literature circles have a lot more fun than what you've been seeing: Tying skill improvement to fun is the hook. Once the kids realize that their discussions could be a lot more interesting and entertaining, they're ready to create their Discussion Skill Table Cards.

Ask groups to create a two-column list. Have them label the left-hand column "Skills That Make Discussion More Fun" and the right-hand column "Skills That Make Discussion More Interesting." Then have groups

Skills That Make Discussion More Fun	Skills That Make Discussion More Interesting
smiling friendliness using names encouraging others to participate recognizing others' contributions	supporting ideas with quotes from the text asking follow-up questions respectfully disagreeing with an idea coming up with different interpretations asking questions about parts that were confusing

brainstorm skills for each column. Make sure everyone writes the brainstorm in their journals so that they can refer to the lists for other mini-lessons. After the group brainstorming, develop a master list with the class. A typical master list will look something like the one shown here.

Once the master list is developed, groups return to the huddle and determine which four or five skills they need most in order to "kick it up a notch." Then each member picks one skill that she wants to be in charge of. From that point on, it's that member's responsibility to model that skill as well as encourage other members to use it. In order to keep these skills at the forefront of the next discussion, each student creates a table card.

Give each student an eight-by-five-inch index card. Have students fold the card in half lengthwise, with the blank side facing out. On one side of the fold they write the skill in big letters. This side will face out as a reminder to

Table Card Backsides

Thoughtful Questions
- "What does that illustration make you think about?"
- "How do you feel about that passage?"
- "What are some connections with this passage?"
- "What was your favorite part in this reading?"

Friendliness and Support
- "You must be butter because you are on a roll!"
- "You are on fire, _____!"
- "That was A+ quality, _____!"
- "Come on _____, your group is behind you!"
- "We believe in you, _____!"

---

the other members to use that skill. On the other side of the fold facing the "skill owner," the student writes four or five specific phrases he could use in the next literature circle discussion to model that skill. In the examples, you'll notice that some kids chose serious academic skills while others decided to have some fun—which is one of our goals, right? In the "Friendliness and Support" example, I know we never would have brainstormed, "You must be butter because you are on a roll!" However, silly as that line was, the group owned it and used it enthusiastically; plus, they had a lot of laughs. More important, because the kids enjoyed being together and became more invested in each other, their conversation about their book improved. As long as the table cards are positive and reflect the skill, minimal teacher intervention is required.

After making the cards, students display them and refer to them for the remainder of their literature circle discussions.

Working the Room

As you circulate through the classroom, require groups to set the cards up where other members can see them. However, don't be overly concerned if you still do not observe stellar skill usage. Changing behavior takes time. If

you see great skill usage, mention it to the group on the spot and encourage them to keep it up. Or, if that seems too intrusive, jot yourself notes so that you can go back to each group as discussion is winding down and give them some positive feedback.

You'll also notice that, when given a choice, students will tend to focus more on the "making discussion fun" skills versus the "making discussion interesting" skills. Though we teachers always want the kids to dig deeper into the text, the main reward for students to meet in a literature circle is a social one, so it makes sense that they choose skills that will help everyone get along and enjoy each other's company. For positive group dynamics, these "frivolous" skill choices are actually very sound. If members of a group do not treat each other well, they will not even bother to prepare for the discussion, let alone analyze the text. Once students have mastered the "fun" skills, they willingly work on the other skills with minimal prodding from us.

Reflecting

After each group discussion, have students compare which skills were used the most and which ones were ignored. Based on their conclusions, groups then make a plan for improving the use of the weaker skills in the next discussion. Students also need to examine how using the skills changed their discussion. They will often observe that the time went by faster, everyone got more involved, discussion was more fun and lively, or they ended up talking about some of the topics longer than they expected. Discussing these positive changes in a quick whole-class discussion is important because it demonstrates that using these skills really does make a difference.

What Can Go Wrong?

From our experience, two problems can arise. First, there is always one joker in the group who will write insulting phrases on his table card just to see if the teacher is paying attention. In defense, you can have kids create the cards the day before discussion and skim through them before they are used. Check out the "Using Names" example. Yes, every statement uses a member's name, but . . .

Sometimes a member will have good intentions, but the statements come out all wrong—as you can see in the Staying on Task example.

Whenever you discuss social skill phrases, it's important to emphasize using positive statements. It's amazing how quickly a few nasty words can shut down a group permanently. If members feel threatened, they will not share their ideas and feelings. In the case of the student who wrote the "Staying on

Table Cards—Using Names

- "Julie, you really stink; did you forget to use deodorant?"
- "Michelle, the stench is just flowing off you."
- "Everyone clap for Kevin; he showered!"
- "Lori, you don't stink, you smell. Maybe the reek is coming from Julie. I dunno; is it you Kevin?"

Table Cards—Staying on Task

- "Shut up!"
- "Let's hurry up and get this done."
- "None of us care what you did over the weekend!"

Table Cards—Staying on Task (New and Improved)

- "Let's hear everyone's ideas one at a time."
- "We have twenty minutes for discussion. What do you want to start with?"
- "Let's talk about our notes first and then our weekends."

Task" cards, the goal behind the statements is legitimate: She just needs a private mini-lesson in changing the wording.

What's Next?

After the kids seem to have mastered their table card skills, have them trade skills. Usually students take ownership of the skill with which they are most comfortable. Trading cards stretches them to hone social skills that are not within their repertoire. Or, have whole groups exchange cards. No two groups ever choose the same social skills, so this is another good way to help kids practice some different components of good conversation.

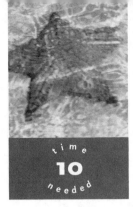

time
10
needed

Getting More Mileage Out of Drawings

Why Do It?

We've mentioned several times that drawing in response to a book often brings new topics, questions, and visions to the table. But we have to guide, even police, the use of illustrations if we want them to work. First, the "left-brained" kids typically blow off this part of the literature circle preparation. Coming up with a good illustration is just as important as the written responses because drawing requires the brain to work in a different way. For many students, doing an illustration stretches their thinking in new directions. Second, when students have put a lot of effort into their illustrations, it is disappointing to see these masterpieces get such short shrift. The kids hold them up, someone says, "Oh that's when . . . ," the other kids nod in agreement, and the discussion of that illustration is over! Here's a lesson for helping students extend the discussion of their illustrations.

Teaching the Lesson

Getting Started

Getting more mileage out of illustrations requires the group to break their discussion of each illustration into two rounds, much like the earlier strategy in this chapter, Save the Last Word for Me.

154 ■ CHAPTER 5 REFINING DISCUSSION SKILLS

Responding to an Illustration

- Explain what is going on with other characters during the same time as the scene in the illustration.
- Explain how this picture relates back to something that happened earlier in the story.
- Imagine a change of story events and then explain how the picture would change.
- Describe how you imagined this scene as you read. What did you see differently than the artist?

In round one, the artist displays his illustration proudly and each student says something about it. The problem with this is that by the time it's the fourth member's turn to speak, all of the obvious things have been said. So, students need to brainstorm what else the picture suggests that isn't so obvious. Have students brainstorm in their literature circle groups first and then get together for a master list that becomes part of their journals. The figure shows some of the new ideas for responding to an illustration.

In round two, each member gets to ask the artist a question about his illustration. Of course, the kids will automatically respond with, "What's there to ask after we each explained?" Au contraire! Send the kids back to their groups to brainstorm and then make a second master list of questions. The next figure shows what one class came up with.

1. Why did you choose that character to draw?

2. What interested you about this part of the story?

3. Where was this in the story? What passage would you use as a caption?

4. What details would you have added if you had more time?

5. What feelings does this scene show?

6. What's another part of the story that would make a good illustration?

7. Which details in your drawing are most important to the story?

8. If you were a great artist, what scene would you have illustrated instead?

9. How does your illustration show symbolism, irony, or a moral?

10. If you became a new character in the story, where would you be in this drawing?

Once the class has brainstormed ways to extend responses and artist questions, students should use their lists during their next literature circle discussion. Of course, during discussion but *after* all others have contributed, the artist can add her own thoughts that the group did not unearth.

Working the Room

The main thing to watch for is that the groups follow the two-rounds protocol. In other words, each person takes a turn at contributing an idea *and* asking the artist a question.

Reflecting

At the end of discussion, ask groups to list three things that changed in their conversation about these latest illustrations. Usually students will notice that by the time they finished discussing the illustrations, they had actually covered a lot of the topics from their written notes, questions, or chosen passages. See, a picture *is* worth a thousand words! Also, the kids find that discussing the illustrations in depth can be just plain fun.

What Can Go Wrong?

The only thing that drags this activity down is when kids produce really anemic illustrations. Usually this involves just a few kids, so it's best to pull them aside for a private chat. Most of the time the illustrations do improve after that. Also, illustrations tend to get better once students realize they are not a "throw-away" part of the discussion preparation.

Another problem we've run into occasionally is the R- or X-rated drawing. Nancy once discovered an artist who was definitely pushing the envelope. When confronted (the drawing could have been interpreted as sexual harassment), his defense was that he was only illustrating a scene from the book. So now we say:

Since some of you are reading adult books that depict adult situations, you need to remember that this is school. Therefore, your drawings need to be suitable for all audiences. You are like movie reviewers. Even though many films nowadays are R-rated, they still need to write or talk about the films in a tasteful manner. A movie reviewer who wants to keep his job might reference an adult scene, but he will not describe it in graphic, colorful detail.

Variations

Start an illustration gallery. Display drawings from the different book titles together and encourage the class to take a look at what's going on in the other literature circles. Hopefully, the illustrations will muster interest in reading some of the other books.

chapter 6

Solving Problems:
Students and Groups
Who Struggle

One of the adorable things about teachers is that we don't think like regular human beings. If someone describes a new classroom activity to us—literature circles, for example—we immediately start worrying about the three or five kids in our class who will *not* immediately thrive in this kind of structure. While normal people say, "Hmmm, that's cool, something that works 80 or 90 percent of the time, right out of the box," we already have visions of chaos dancing in our heads.

We imagine Brenda sauntering in, not having done the reading for the seventeenth day in a row; Jerry's response log filled with four-letter words; the group in the corner talking about the football game (except when we hover directly behind them); "Mr. Funtime" stealing Jane's platform shoes and voguing around for all to admire. (We mention these particular scenarios because each of them, and worse, has actually happened to us.)

Yes, we teachers worry a lot about the problem students, the outliers, the ones who struggle, the kids who don't fit—or won't fit. We're big-hearted people; that's why we chose this profession. When even the most cynical politician declaims, "Every child can learn," we get teary-eyed. Of course, we're the ones who have to make good on that motto—and it's not easy. There are a wide range of reading levels and academic abilities in any classroom, even if it's called "honors English." Kids come to us with hurts we didn't cause and can't salve, but that affect the classroom weather every day. And those diabolical schedulers always put one kid in each of our classes for whom school is, to put it mildly, *just not their thing*.

No wonder we worry when "experts" try to sell us on activities that decentralize the classroom, put the kids in charge, and turn the teacher into a facilitator! But these bugaboos we fear, these scary management problems, are actually normal, predictable, and to a great extent solvable. So we're glad to offer this selection of problem-solving mini-lessons, aimed at the most common and worrisome issues that plague book clubs:

- dealing with students who don't do the work
- meeting the needs of special education students
- getting shy members to speak up
- helping dominant members step back
- steering wandering groups back on task
- showing groups how to get through "lulls"
- making sure members don't give away book endings
- working with groups that want to give up on a book

Armed with these lessons, you can push through most of the predictable problems that might otherwise test your faith.

We're not promising perfection—we teach real students, too, and we never get 100 percent. But a great majority of garden-variety stumbling blocks can be overcome, potholes averted, and sidetracks bypassed. These problem-solving strategies help us expect more of students, set higher standards, and insist that they steadily grow as readers and group members. Just as with parenting, you've got to give responsibility to get responsibility, and that always involves some risk. Kids need chances to practice activities at their own developmental level, get feedback, and try again. The benefits are huge—when young people learn to operate in this kind of group, they're gaining a life skill of major significance. And if some of them fall in love with books along the way, what's not to like?

time
20
needed

Books on Tape

Why Do It?

If you have a heterogeneous, mixed-ability classroom (and who doesn't?) or you have mainstreamed special education students, you will need books on tape as one accommodation (along with properly leveled book choices) for students who read slowly or struggle. Happily, almost all the popular books for teenage readers, both classics and young adult (YA) literature, are now available on inexpensive, well-produced audiotapes and CDs. The same device that many adult readers enjoy in their cars can be the tool that allows a student with reading problems to join fully in a higher-order conversation about the ideas in a book. Indeed, for kids with learning disabilities in reading, accessing the story via a tape allows them a rare opportunity to shine in the classroom, showing that they can respond, question, connect, speculate, interpret, and judge as well as anyone. For many teachers, this is another reason for providing in-class reading time for literature circle books—to make sure that kids who are using books on tape are getting to the listening station, keeping up, and getting the support they need.

But books on tape aren't just for struggling readers; they can add a new dimension for everyone, especially when the books are read by a strong performer or, more rarely, the original author. So, this mini-lesson is for everyone, both to destigmatize the tape users in the class and to introduce a valuable variation. We also see it as another iteration of the Savoring Powerful Language mini-lesson in the next chapter.

162   ■   CHAPTER 6   SOLVING PROBLEMS: STUDENTS AND GROUPS WHO STRUGGLE

Teaching the Lesson

Getting Started

Choose a favorite book on tape, one that's read by a great actor. We especially enjoy:

Hatchet by Gary Paulsen, read by Peter Coyote

Maniac McGee by Jerry Spinelli, read by S. Epatha Merkerson (of TV's *Law and Order*)

Harry Potter books by J. K. Rowling, read by Jim Dale

Monster by Walter Dean Meyers, read by a full cast

Esperanza Rising by Pam Munoz Ryan, read by Trini Alvarado

Speak by Laurie Halse Anderson, read by Mandy Sigfried

Holes by Louis Sachar, read by Kerry Beyer

Locate a two- or three-minute segment that is vivid, important, or memorable. Photocopy this section of the book for everyone in the class and distribute the handouts.

Have students read the segment quietly, thinking about how the passage might be read out loud. Next, ask for a volunteer to read aloud a paragraph or two. Then ask, "Who has another interpretation?" Get one or two more students to offer their own renderings of the piece. Prod additional volunteers with cues like, "Who has a completely different idea of how to read this?"

Then play the professional version. Let everyone enjoy it, and then conduct some discussion:

Did the reader sound like you expected? What was alike and different about his [or her] interpretation from some of ours? Did the reading aloud change your picture of or thinking about the story? How is hearing the book different from reading it? Would you want to use books on tape as part of your experience of a book? How might it fit in for you?

As you send students off for their book club meetings, suggest that they spend the first few minutes letting volunteers read aloud important passages from the day's reading. (Obviously, be careful not to put the struggling readers on the spot with this assignment.)

Working the Room

This is mainly a demonstration and back-to-work lesson. Just visit groups when they begin their meetings, listening in as they read aloud to each other. If you offer in-class reading time before or after book club meetings (or on alternating days), check in with the kids who are using books on tape. Also, compare notes regularly with the special education teacher who is assigned to your classroom or (we hope) comes by often.

Reflecting

If you have encouraged all students to listen to a chapter or two as they read a book, it is important to talk about the impact of that experience. When students have almost finished their reading, it's a good time to have a debriefing session and ask: "How have the tapes influenced your understanding or enjoyment of the books?" We often find that the tapes help kids to really "hear" the writer's voice as they read, spark an interest in researching the author's life, or just build the habit of listening to books on tape, as another form of "pleasure reading."

What Can Go Wrong?

Obviously, we don't want skillful readers to be listening to entire books on tape, one after the other. And even for kids who struggle, it's better to alternate between reading and listening, even if the reading segments are necessarily short. Some teachers like to have students follow along in the text as the tape plays; others, feeling the kids need to "get lost in the story" just like fluent readers do, don't enforce this policy.

You may not have tapes for every book your students might choose—then what? As with books, building a classroom library of tapes is a multiyear effort, the work of a whole career, really. Just start now—you'll be amazed how fast things accumulate and how long your tentacles really are.

If some students pick a book for which no tape exists, what a wonderful project for those kids in the drama class to work on between musicals! They can make you a custom tape, throw in some super production values, and maybe even get some extra credit. Or, if university students come to your school for required "observation hours," ask if they have time to help out with an important literacy project—and hand them a microphone!

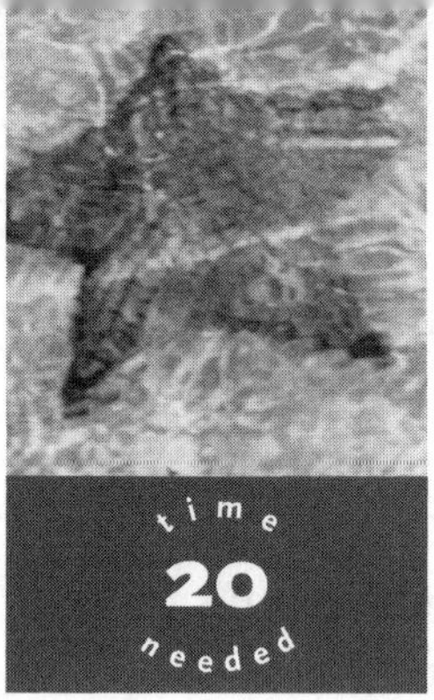
time
20
needed

Dealing with Slackers and Unprepared Members

Why Do It?

No matter how great the books are in your literature circles and no matter how well you've trained your students for peer-led group discussion, some members will still come unprepared. Rather than meting out consequences yourself, we've found it much more beneficial to let the groups deal with this problem. Though we're certainly not economists, we sometimes think of well-prepared students as "assets" to book clubs, and unprepared slackers as "liabilities." Once poor preparation rears its ugly head, it's time for student groups to determine their own "liability policies" for handling members who don't do the reading or prepare any discussion notes.

Teaching the Lesson

Getting Started

We introduce the lesson this way:

> *We've noticed that unprepared members have been bogging down the discussions lately. It's easy to recognize unprepared members because*

they're not looking at the book, they haven't brought any notes, and their conversations tend to be on topics other than the text. To solve this problem, your literature circle groups need to brainstorm ways to productively deal with members who come unprepared.

Tell groups to work together for about five minutes; then regroup to create a whole-class master list, which, as usual, gets recorded in the journals. The list on the next page shows the ways Nancy's American Studies class thought unprepared members might participate—or not.

Since liabilities are a problem the groups must handle, we cross out any items that shift responsibility back to the teacher: All solutions require that the group own the problem. Once students have a variety of choices in front of them, they decide what will work best for their book club and commit to that decision.

Besides determining the initial rules, we also ask each group to come up with two corollaries. First, will the liability policy change if the same member repeatedly comes unprepared? Some groups establish tougher consequences for repeat offenders; other groups stick with a one-level policy. Second, what unobtrusive visual symbol will show the teacher that a student is a liability today? After all, you may want to observe the discussion and even award points for participation without having to ask, "Okay, who doesn't have their reading and notes done?" Most groups decide that a liability member must label himself by wearing a sticky note on the shoulder or straddling his chair so that the back faces the group. Ouch, sounds like a tough stigma, but it's no worse than the teacher coming around with a clipboard and making the slackers confess out loud, one at a time.

Working the Room

Be sure that each group gives you a copy of its liability policy and visual signal, written on an index card. That way, as you observe you can see if the kids' policy is working. The index cards are also a handy place for you to make notes on the group's skills and interactions.

Students' Suggestions for Ways Unprepared Members Can Participate in Group Meetings

- Listen but not talk.
- Listen carefully and take notes on the discussion.
- Does not participate in discussion but looks for information/reads passages we are discussing.
- Apologize to the group and explain why they are a liability. Can only participate in discussion by asking questions.
- Work as an observer, listening carefully and writing down the starter and follow-up questions the group members ask. Go over questions after finishing the reading assignment.
- Listen carefully to discussion but not participate. The liability is in charge of collecting papers and turning them in.
- Liabilities can write on the board "I want to be in the discussion group" a hundred times. Then they can discuss with the teacher why they didn't do their homework.
- Liabilities can listen to discussion and act as timekeeper and also make sure everyone stays on task. They can also help put the chairs away.
- Liabilities should be punished, have to do the assignment but still get a zero.
- Listen silently and then make comments/ask questions during the last few minutes of the discussion. Group can help explain story to them based on questions.
- Liabilities form new groups for the day and talk about the book they're reading and discuss the assignment however best they can.
- Sit separate, finish the reading/work, join group if discussion is not over.
- Listen silently but carefully observe and record the conversation skills the group is using.
- Contribute on parts of reading that they covered but sit silently and listen to the discussion on the parts they didn't finish.

Reflecting

After each discussion, groups should review and possibly revise their reading schedule if an unrealistic calendar is producing the liabilities. Indeed, anytime members fall into liability status, the group needs to find out why they were unprepared and help them come up with a plan for better performance the next time.

On a day when all of the members in all of the groups have come prepared, have a class celebration after the discussions are over. Structure your debriefing that day so that students can testify how great discussions are when all members are full participants.

What Can Go Wrong?

First, students sometimes will come up with goofy choices for the visual liability symbol. One group of boys decided to place their sticky notes on their crotches rather than their shoulders. They had to rethink that decision—fast! Another group decided that any liabilities would have to sing "The Barney Song" while dancing. Since Nancy thought that might be amusing to witness, she said nothing. Later, when she saw a guilty student wearing the customary sticky note, she asked about the song and dance. As it turned out, one member slipped the song idea under the wire unbeknownst to the rest of the group.

Second, though turning the problem back to the group helps increase the chances that students will feel more obligated to their peers and come prepared, it will never eliminate the problem entirely. When the kids get lazy, collecting everyone's notes for the latest discussion and grading them is a good old-fashioned way to increase preparation compliance. However, that's a lot of work, so we recommend it as a last resort. Try first to watch for the repeat offenders and have a private chat to see what's going on.

Third, sometimes groups forget about their policies. If that's the case, build a "liability check" into the meeting agenda and have members declare their particular status and their personal plans for that day's contributions.

Surprisingly, we seldom see fellow members covering up for slackers. When kids have put in the time to read and prepare for a good discussion, they tend to be annoyed by unreliable members who aren't pulling their weight.

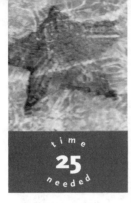

Sharing Airtime: Helping Dominant or Shy Members

Why Do It?

Unequal participation is a common problem in any group discussion. Think about the last committee meeting you attended in your district. Did everyone get to speak or was the floor dominated by just a few members? Probably the latter, though most committees would generate better ideas and solutions if everybody participated. Just because some people are quiet that doesn't mean their ideas are any less valuable. The same holds for literature circle discussions. Students who dominate a discussion need to learn how to hold back a bit, while those who are shy need to be recognized and encouraged.

Teaching the Lesson

Getting Started

Before students go into their groups, have them pull out their journals and list all of the book club members, including themselves. Then tell them to rank each member in order of how much they talk in the group. Number one is the person who talks the most and number five is the person who talks the least.

Next, have the students get into their literature circles and tell them that they'll be working to ensure more even participation and also practicing follow-up questions. Pass out five "chips" to each student. These chips can be

poker chips or just small squares of paper or cardboard. Each group should assign one member of the group to be the banker. Give the bankers a plastic cup (the kind they sell at the Dollar Store or that people are always trying to get rid of at garage sales). The cup makes the banker more "official" and gives her the "authority" to make sure the Talking Chip rules are followed.

During the group discussion, each student must turn in one of the Talking Chips each time she gives an answer or opinion. Once all of a member's chips are turned in, she can no longer give answers. However, that member can still ask follow-up questions or bring up a new topic for her notes. When the treasurer has collected all of the chips, then redistributed to the members and a new round of discussion is.

Ideally, after a couple of rounds, students begin to recognize their discussion patterns and try to adjust. The member who always holds back realizes that it is easier to jump into the discussion earlier rather than waiting until everyone else's chips are gone and then having the group focus all of its attention on her. Likewise, the member who loses all his chips early and has to ask twenty-five follow-up questions before he can offer another opinion learns to hold back some answers and maybe start asking other members questions instead.

Working the Room

The main thing to look for here is that students are following the directions. Someone will probably ask if he can turn in his chips for one-word or yes/no answers. Tell him no. The low-level participants cannot get off the hook so easily.

Reflecting

After the discussion, have the students go back to the group member list in their journals and share how they had originally ranked each other's participation level. This can be interesting because different individual perceptions lead to different rankings. Before using the chips, the group's biggest talker might not even be aware she is hogging airtime, while this pattern of behavior stands out in day-glo orange to the teacher and the other members.

Next, have the group examine how the discussion changed when using the Talking Chips. Students often notice that discussion slows down, because everyone now has to think about what they're going to say and whether it's worth a chip. Further, groups often find that the quietest member, the one who was seldom heard from in past discussions, has some pretty good ideas. Groups also typically report that they had to ask more follow-up questions in order to help others use up their chips so that a new round could be started.

What Can Go Wrong?

Because the chips slow down conversations and drastically alter the typical discussion patterns within a group, members often complain that the chips are interfering with their discussion. Ironically, the most vocal complainers are usually the ones who routinely monopolize the conversation. Hold fast to your resolve and have the groups use the chips for the rest of that day's discussion. You'll notice that after the nonstop talkers lose all their chips a couple of times, they start to hold back a bit and contribute more evenly. Nancy recently observed a girl who previously talked *all the time,* sitting with a pile of chips in front of her while listening carefully to the comments of her group members.

The worst thing that can go wrong is that the kids will go nuts and start throwing chips around the room. Usually the root cause of such aberrant behavior is that unprepared group members have nothing else to do but entertain themselves with off-task behavior. As always, it's a good idea to assess preparedness before passing out any chips.

What's Next?

The Talking Chips lesson is one that can be repeated several times depending on how much practice groups need in evening out their participation. You can also use this strategy to focus on improving the group's follow-up questioning. In this case, members gets three or four chips each. When it is their turn to present a discussion item to the group, students have to ask a follow-up question and get it answered for each of the chips, which are turned in to the banker. Once the chips are used up, it is the next member's turn to direct a topic. Each member must take a turn directing a topic and using up his question chips.

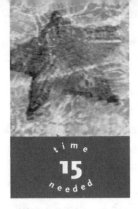

Overcoming Off-Task Triggers

time needed **15**

Why Do It?

Any group of people will get off-task sooner or later, usually sooner. A little off-task discussion is actually good because it lends some fun and playfulness to the group—"social lubrication," as they call it in the field of group dynamics. However, constant off-task behavior interferes with the academic job at hand. Plus, when groups engage in extended irrelevant digressions, the discussion usually does not reflect equal participation. Instead, a couple of students just talk on, shutting out the other members. So, not only does lengthy off-task discussion disrupt the mission of book clubs, it also upsets the harmonious relationship that needs to be maintained between members. If you observe recurrent off-task discussion in literature circles, it is important to help groups examine the triggers that lead to those behaviors.

Teaching the Lesson

Getting Started

Start by describing some of the off-task behaviors you've observed in past literature circle meetings and explain that a little of this is natural, but a lot impedes discussion. Then have students turn to a new sheet in their journals and fold the page to create three columns. They should label the first column "Off-Task Behavior," the second column "Behavior Trigger," and the third column "Solution."

Next, have students gather in their groups and brainstorm the different kinds of off-task behaviors their group is guilty of. Besides talking about topics other than the text, they might mention talking to other groups, whistling, or tossing the book in the air.

After they've listed these behaviors, students go to the middle column and figure out what triggers these off-task behaviors. Off-topic discussion, for example, might be triggered by something in the book that reminds them of something else. Whistling or book tossing might be the result of coming unprepared or being ignored by the rest of the group. The next figure shows one group's chart.

After students have determined the triggers, they need to come up with some solutions. Remind the groups that they should consider ways to avoid the behavior, ways to recognize it, and ways for getting back on track.

Once students set up their plans, they can try them out in a discussion. Typically, just recognizing what gets a group off task helps keep them on track.

Working the Room

Watch for off-task behavior, but when it happens, do nothing at first. See if the group can self-correct. If the problem continues, intervene by asking the group to review their off-task behavior list and then ask them what their plan was. The more a group has enjoyed being off-task, the more reluctant the kids will be to change. These are the groups you will need to monitor more closely.

Reflecting

After the discussion, students should review their plans, see how they worked, and decide whether they need to add or change anything. If time permits, have groups share their off-task problems and solutions with the class. This gives everyone the chance to see that groups are usually more similar than different. It also offers groups a wider range of solutions in case their original plans didn't work very well. Remember to have the kids review their Off-Task Behavior Charts before each discussion.

Off-Task Behavior Chart

Off-Task Behavior	Behavior Trigger	Solution
Talking about stuff that has nothing to do with the book	Starts with a connection but then gets off track	Assign a different person each discussion to remind the group to return to the book.
Throwing book in air	Bored Left out of conversation	Tell member to open up to page being discussed. Keep everyone involved in the conversation.
Talking to another group	Bored left out of conversation	Put more effort into Membership Grid [?] so that we get to know each other better. keep everyone involved in the conversation.
Finishing Discussion Notes during discussion	Unprepared	Remind members of homework a couple days before it's due.

What Can Go Wrong?

Sometimes off-task behavior stems from more serious problems than just getting off the topic. First, a group will continue to be off-task if members are not committed to each other. If a group has not bonded, members are likely to be unprepared for discussion and, even if they are, show little interest in what the others have to say. In such cases, it's best to return to those lessons in Chapter 2 that help set the foundation for a more positive learning community.

The other time that a group will seriously and continually go off-task is when they've all decided that they hate the book. Of course, they chose the book, but that becomes moot. When this happens, you'll have to step in and negotiate. If there is still enough time, suggest an alternative title that you think might be more appealing. Our Abandoning a Book mini-lesson at the end of this chapter offers procedures for this. But sometimes you can cajole a group into sticking out the book and giving a better performance by promising to help them get their number one picks for the next literature circle. Be sure you keep your promises! Also, now that you know these kids are "tough customers," you'll be able to steer them toward titles that will work better for them in the future.

time
10
needed

Extending Discussion When You've Run Out of Stuff on Your Notes but the Clock Is Still Running

Why Do It?

If you notice that most of your groups are finishing five or ten minutes before the end of the designated discussion time, you may need to repeat some of the earlier lessons on questioning or preparing good notes. However, if a different group finishes early each time, setting up a discussion-stretching backup plan is in order. That way, when the kids complete their conversation more quickly than usual, they'll still be able to talk about the book for the allotted time.

Teaching the Lesson

Getting Started

Before the literature circles meet, explain that you've noticed that groups sometimes finish early and then have nothing to talk about. Have the students pull out their journals and brainstorm some answers to this question: "When a group finishes early, what are some topics or questions members

Questions to Extend Discussion

1. What's your favorite part from the story so far?
2. Based on what we've read so far, how do you think it's going to end?
3. Who is your favorite character? Why?
4. Everyone rereads a page and finds a new passage or vocabulary word to share/discuss.
5. What do you think the author thought about or experienced in order to write this story?
6. How do you feel about the story now compared to when we first started reading it?
7. Look through the text for literary devices: simile, metaphor, irony, symbolism, alliteration. After everyone finds one, discuss them.
8. What advice would you give each of the characters?
9. If this story were made into a movie or television show, how would the story need to be changed?
10. If this story were made into a movie, how would you cast the characters?
11. Pull out the Membership Grid and discuss the earlier topic again, except this time the members have to do the interview as if they were one of the characters in the novel.

---

could discuss in order to keep talking about the book?" After a couple of minutes, compile the results on an overhead while the class jots down any new ideas. (Questions to Extend Discussion shows some common responses.)

Now that members are armed with their backup lists, they proceed with their literature circle discussions as usual. The kids' regular notes might carry them through the discussion, but if a shortfall occurs, they now have other topics to use.

Working the Room

The biggest reason groups finish early is not that members don't have good notes, but that they failed to pursue the discussion topics thoroughly. As you move about the classroom, remind students to ask follow-up questions and perhaps use the Save the Last Word for Me strategy discussed in Chapter 5. Also, the kids' books should be open! Discussion always goes dangerously fast when the book never gets cracked.

Reflecting

After the literature circle discussions, find out which groups used the backup questions and which didn't. Ask groups that didn't use the questions to reflect and report back on how they got more mileage out of their notes. Have the groups that did use the questions reflect and report on which questions were most fun to discuss and why. Also, after a few discussions, have students return to their backup questions and add new ideas.

What Can Go Wrong?

Once in a while you're going to run into a truly dysfunctional group. No lesson is going to improve their discussion performance and personal interaction if other issues are standing in the way. They will finish their required discussion as quickly as possible and not be interested in asking any further questions. Rather than trying to nag and cajole them into better performance, settle for civil behavior that doesn't distract other groups. Observe the members carefully and try to figure out why they work together so poorly. If you can do it discreetly, pull the members aside individually and interview them; you might learn things that you would never have guessed on your own. Keep the information to yourself, but remember to use it when setting up the next literature circle groups.

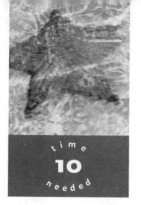

Don't Spoil the Ending

Why Do It?

One of the most annoying things a book club member can do is finish the book early and then blab the ending, spoiling the book for everyone else. How rude! Even if innocent overflowing enthusiasm is the cause of such disclosures, it's still a buzz-killer for everybody else. Even TV movie critics are careful not to give away plot twists and surprise endings. But let's not get too upset. The resolution of plotlines is not the only payoff for reading a book, and kids' reading lives won't end if they have to finish a book with somebody else's "prediction" in their heads. Still, it's nicer to keep everyone on the same page if we can, unfolding the story together.

This mini-lesson is based on the dictum "you can read ahead, but you can't talk ahead." When literature circles first meet, the members set up a schedule that lays out the specific chapters and pages to be read for each meeting. (See Making a Reading Calendar in Chapter 4.) It's important for the group to stick to this schedule or, if people want to slow down or accelerate, to make any changes by group consensus. But that covers only the group meetings. Individuals may decide to read the book faster than the baseline schedule, for many good reasons. Maybe a kid falls in love with the book and just cannot put it down: That's an experience (possibly a life-changing one) we do not want to quash. If our main purpose for doing lit circles, after all, is to get kids to join the Big Book Club, the one that lasts your whole life, those hooked-on-a-book experiences are to be treasured. Or perhaps a student has scheduling problems, tons of other homework, or upcoming projects, and needs to cram the book in around those commitments. Whatever the reason, it's not "wrong" to read ahead. But it is definitely wrong to talk ahead.

Teaching the Lesson

....
Getting Started

This is a perfect problem for the baseline mini-lesson structure outlined in Chapter 10. We start by saying:

I've noticed that some people are reading ahead in their books—which is fine. But sometimes they have blurted out details or events from chapters that the rest of the group hasn't read yet. This can really take the edge off for other readers. So what can we do? Who's got some ideas about specific, concrete actions we can take to solve this problem?

Here's what one class brainstormed:

- Make a rule—no talking ahead.
- Keep the books in the classroom, so we can't take them home.
- Tear the books into sections to match them to our reading calendar.
- Make ourselves a table card. Don't blab!!
- If you read ahead, look at the group calendar before the meeting—remind yourself where in the story we're supposed to stop.
- Tell the group you read ahead and ask them to shut you up right away if you start wrecking the book.

Some of these ideas are clearly more workable than others. Tearing the book into fifths and doling out one chunk at a time is certainly not an option in any school we know of. But the last two have promise—they just need a little shaping by the teacher. (This is a good reminder that soliciting kids' ideas on a classroom management issue doesn't mean that you have to accept them unmodified; you certainly have a right to suggest ideas that you know will work.)

So we add one more "stopper" to the list for the read-ahead kids. "If you decide to read ahead of your group's schedule, you must put a rubber band around the part of the book the other kids haven't read yet. This only works if you look really carefully at the text first, noting the dividing line between the stuff everyone has read and the place where you went ahead." Oh, and if you have visions of students shooting each other's eyes out during a no-holds-barred rubber band war, stock up on big colored paper clips. They'll serve the same purpose, and straightening out the clips in order to poke classmates isn't quite as irresistible as snapping a rubber band across the room.

Now that you've added your idea to the mix, let the groups review the list of options and decide how they are going to handle the "reading ahead" problem.

Working the Room

This mini-lesson doesn't lead to much same-day action, except for the couple of kids who might have read ahead and their groups. Head for those book clubs, and make sure that the group is affirming a policy and procedure.

Reflecting

The rubber band works amazingly well—it's a tangible marker, an effective reminder, and a little bit of a status symbol. If lots of books with rubber-banded sections start popping up around your classroom, you can pat your-self on the back for a mini-lesson well done. It may also indicate that you've got great, irresistible titles loose in your classroom and for this, again, con-gratulations. But this might also be a sign that kids are scheduling their books too slowly, setting their day-to-day number of pages too low. If lots of students are forging ahead, it may be time to renegotiate the reading calendar for everyone—or at the very least, think about shortening up the next cycle of book clubs in your classroom. This is one trend we are recognizing in our own teaching: We now move kids through books faster than we used to. Where once we would allow three weeks or more for a cycle of literature cir-cles, we now do some in about two weeks. This may mean that we're picking books of greater interest or simply reflect our realization that dragging out a book doesn't help anyone.

What do you do when a kid does finish a book early—days and days early? Some teachers believe that when a kid finishes ahead of schedule, she should pick up some other reading, perhaps an independent book. This is based on the "norm of continuous work" that you see in true workshop-style classrooms. In writing workshop, we don't allow kids who wrote a really long story yesterday to take today off, saying, "I finished my writing." Instead, we smile at them and say, "No, you didn't. In workshop, we use *all* the time available to work on our writing. You have lots of choices—you can start a new piece, edit an old one, make an illustration, work on your portfolio. But you can't 'be done' with writing, today or any day." So maybe it's the same with reading; we're never done. If you finish one book, start another.

Good-hearted teachers disagree on this one. Some feel that if a kid reads a whole book really fast, we're "punishing" them if we require them to read another. Maybe they'll start lying, pretending they're not reading ahead, and set off a whole new wave of dysfunctional behavior. Maybe we should just let them use this "found time" to catch up on their math homework. Reasonable arguments on both sides: your call.

What Can Go Wrong?

Even with the best warnings, mechanisms, and consequences in place, occasionally kids (much like adults) will still blurt out important details or that surprise ending. This must be some primordial defect of the species. We bet that thousands of years ago there were Neanderthals who would stand at cave entrances and reveal the contents of the final paintings as people entered. "They both die in the end," blabs Blog. Bummer.

time
10
needed

Abandoning a Book

Why Do It?

This mini-lesson comes up naturally the first time a book club asks your permission to give up on a book they've started. And this *will* happen, guaranteed. Thoughtful teachers have different approaches to this problem. Some believe that finishing a book you do not totally love can be a character-building experience. After all, school life is full of assigned projects, books we don't want to read, and activities we don't want to do. Other teachers, perhaps recognizing how often they give up on books themselves, prefer to "keep it real" and let kids dump a book like grown-ups commonly do. If you choose this latter policy, the question remains: If a literature circle abandons a book, what do the kids do instead?

Teaching the Lesson

Getting Started

The problem-solving mini-lesson format outlined in Chapter 10 works great for this situation. We identify the problem, develop some solutions with students, and then put them right to work. Here's how we start:

> *One group recently approached me about dropping their lit circle book, and I thought this would be a good time for us to talk this over. What happens when you've picked the wrong book and you just don't want*

to finish it? What should be our policy about this? Take a few minutes and talk this over in your book clubs, and we'll get back together.

Give the students three to four minutes, then ask for their suggestions about "abandoned book" procedures. If your students are like ours, some groups will recommend a hard-nosed "you made your bed, now lie in it" approach, while others will support a laissez-faire extreme. But you'll probably have plenty of suggestions that reflect an underlying belief that if you drop a book, you shouldn't get a big chunk of recess instead. You've got to do something else, something valuable, with that freed-up reading and discussion time.

Use the combined suggestions to fashion a class policy centered on the idea that "we're always reading and talking about books in literature circles." Here's the policy we developed with one recent class, in which all groups had previously agreed to a common end date for the current round of books. A master Abandoned Book Report is included in the appendix.

Abandoned Book Procedure

The group must fill out an "abandoned book report" and get the teacher's okay.
THEN
Pick another book that's short enough to finish on time, set a new schedule, and get to work.
OR
Decide on some other readings that fit the amount of time remaining for this cycle of book clubs. This might be short stories by the same author, some critical or biographical pieces, or other readings as approved by the teacher.
OR
Pick another book of any length, set a schedule, and meet as much as you can before the class ending date. Then finish the book independently, sharing your responses in dialogue journals or a special meeting.

Working the Room

When you send book clubs off for their regular meeting time, head straight for the group that approached you about abandoning its book. Help the members put the new class-approved procedures right to work, listen to (and probe) their reasons for dropping the book, give them suggestions or alternative titles, and even help them to complete their Abandoned Book Report.

Reflection

There is no immediate need to debrief this mini-lesson, since it affects only one group. You certainly don't want to start an epidemic of abandonment. But a bit later on, it is a good idea to have this club share with the class their whole experience of dropping a book, committing to another, redoing the schedule, and catching up. It's also important for those students to pinpoint what led them to choose the book to begin with so that they don't make the same mistake again, and so that other students continue to give their future book choices the thought they deserve.

What Can Go Wrong?

You might worry that just for the novelty (or the sheer cussedness) of it, a lot of groups will suddenly decide to abandon books if you make it legal. But that has not been our experience. If your classroom library has plenty of great books and the kids have chosen well, they should be pretty well hooked by now.

What if kids suggest a policy that you disapprove of? We remember one group that wanted to skip about half the book and just read the end, because it was too "boring" and they were reading more slowly than planned. ("Boring" often means "hard," in our experience.) We didn't approve the total skip-ahead, but did suggest that the group jigsaw the remaining chapters. Each member was to read and become an expert on just one of the five chapters being read for each meeting. Then, when the group met, each member would give a quick summary, in chapter order, before the general discussion ensued.

Chapter 7

Examining the Author's Craft

In Chapter 1, we expressed our concern about the overemphasis on literary analysis in English classes. Just to reiterate: We think American students spend too much time dissecting books they don't want to read, and not enough time enjoying books they choose for themselves. One of the biggest turn-offs to teenage readers—indeed, almost a species-specific aversion—is when we literature teachers try to sell them on deep, hidden metaphors that they just don't see. We grownups may be right—but how the kids resist our interpretations!

Literary analysis does play an important role in book clubs, as long as we keep it balanced, engaging, and student-centered. So that's just how we handle it here, with five mini-lessons addressing structural elements that really matter, including:

setting

plot development

characterization

theme

language and craft

We usually introduce these literary mini-lessons later in a cycle, after the book clubs are meeting and talking smoothly. Which one we start with depends on the assortment of books in the room. If all groups are reading novels, you can do one on plot, character, or setting. If kids are reading a mixture of fiction and nonfiction books, then a mini-lesson on language or imagery would better cover everyone.

As with all categories of mini-lessons, you can easily make up your own. If you have a literary device that your students must study (personification, simile, whatever), you can design book club mini-lessons around it. Use one of ours as a template; just be sure that all the books being read have ample instances of the device you want to feature.

And here's a "bonus" mini-lesson that we haven't written up, because it's so easy to design yourself. When all the clubs are reading in the same genre (historical novels, mysteries, biographies, self-help books), have them talk and write about this question: "What is the formula for books in this genre? What are the ingredients, the building blocks, the conventions, the stock features of this kind of book?" You can use the lesson-development model in Chapter 10 to flesh out your plan. Obviously, this lesson works best toward the end of a cycle of book clubs, when all ingredients of the genre have come into play.

t i m e

10

n e e d e d

Savoring Powerful Language

Why Do It?

What hooks readers on books for a lifetime? Characters we care about, plots and places we can believe in, ideas that matter to us as human beings. All these are crucial parts of the formula. But what comes first, for many of us, is *language:* We need vivid words, a unique voice, images we can see, taste, feel, smell. We want language that picks us up and puts us down in a whole other place.

We have been struck by what Tim O'Brien has said since being deluged with praise for his magnificent novel *The Things They Carried.* Though many gushing critics (and the Cliff's Notes) relentlessly inventory his gritty Vietnam war details, O'Brien patiently keeps telling people that the book is mostly about "language and words."

If you reflect on your own internal responses to books you really love, you may share our sense that distinctive "language and words" is a nonnegotiable component of excellence in literature. One of the forms of literary response that we rarely mention might be called "savoring"—when we simply marinate ourselves in, wonder at, and reread amazing feats of language. We also notice this hunger for great language in the negative: For those of us who have been avid readers for many years, encountering a book with lackluster language constitutes a prima facie case for abandonment. Life is too short to read books with no voice.

Teaching the Lesson

Getting Started

This lesson is pure simplicity—and pure delight. You just find a passage, maybe a page or two, with great language, and read it aloud to your class. For example, we like to read the poetic and hilarious prologue to Jerry Spinelli's *Maniac McGee*:

> They say Maniac McGee was born in a dump. They say his stomach was a cereal box and his heart a sofa spring. They say he kept an eight-inch cockroach on a leash and that rats stood guard over him while he slept. They say if he was coming and you sprinkled salt on the ground and he ran over it, within two or three blocks he would be as slow as everybody else. They say. What's true? What's myth? It's hard to know. . . . But that's OK. Because the history of a kid is one part fact, two parts legend and three parts snowball. And if you want to know what it was like back when Maniac McGee roamed these parts, well, just run your hand under your movie seat and be very, very careful not to let the facts get mixed up with the truth.

The conversation right after the read-aloud should be natural, informal, and brief. "How did that language strike you?" is as good a prompt as any. We mainly want to send kids into their literature circle discussions with great language ringing in their ears. After kids have commented on the passage for a few minutes, send them off to their regular meetings with this instruction:

> Start your meeting today by looking for some passages of great language in your book. Each member find one section and read it aloud to the group. Talk a little bit about each section. What makes this language special, beautiful, or powerful? When you're done, pick one passage to share with the whole class at debriefing time, and select someone to read it.

Working the Room

The groups have a multistep task here (select, read, comment, take turns), and some will probably benefit from your guidance. You may also have to be a roving volume control, helping kids to adjust their read-aloud level for the group, not the whole classroom.

Reflecting

When you call the kids back from their book club meetings, you can create a bookend to the opening read-aloud. Simply ask the designated student from each group to read the chosen passage aloud. The students will have to focus carefully on the speaker, since most won't have copies of the book to follow along. After each reading, allow for a minute of sink-in time, and then invite comments from listeners. "What did you think? Did that work for you? What made that language special? Did it remind you of any other authors and their style or voice?"

What Can Go Wrong?

Reading aloud to your class is a small performance, and a flat or ill-prepared delivery can send the wrong message to your "audience." You can't just pick a passage and "wing it." You need to practice beforehand, reading the chosen passage out loud several times, and infusing your reading with whatever appropriate dramatic touches you can manage. If this is not something in your normal repertoire, keep this in mind: Teenagers (like most humans) really enjoy being read to. This kind of story-sharing is a universal, primitive rite that goes back to prehistoric campfires and stone circles. You don't need to be a trained thespian to pull this off—just being a book-lover will suffice. You may find yourself falling in love with reading aloud, too.

It's important to have quiet attention for this kind of sensitive performance so that kids can focus completely on your reading. Moreover, you are modeling for them how to read aloud in their own groups. So, don't launch into the read-aloud until your audience is ready.

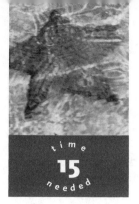

Taking Note of Strong Verbs

Why Do It?

Over the years, we've had the opportunity to hear many different authors speak about their writing. One question that's invariably asked is, "What piece of advice should teachers give to students who are trying to improve their writing?" The most common authorial answer we have heard is that the foundation of good writing is vivid verbs. If all these writers are correct, then having students recognize the strong verbs in their literature circle books can be a springboard to the improvement of their own writing. This mini-lesson embodies exactly what we mean by "reading like a writer."

Teaching the Lesson

Getting Started

Introduce the use of vivid verbs by examining a short excerpt from a novel such as *The Chocolate War* by Robert Cormier. Cormier's prose is filled with strong verbs as he describes Jerry's first day of football practice.

First, just read the example aloud, having the students listen carefully and picture the action. Then pass out photocopies of the passage and tell students to reread silently, circling the verbs that vividly show movement and create a strong mental picture of the action. After a few minutes, have some volunteers share a word they circled and explain why they chose it.

Then have students move into their literature circles and practice acting out each of the circled verbs physically. Finally, regroup as a class and have

The Chocolate War Excerpt

On the third play, he was hit simultaneously by three of them: one, his knees; another, his stomach; a third, his head—the helmet no protection at all. His body seemed to telescope into itself but all the parts didn't fit, and he was stunned by the knowledge that pain isn't just one thing—it is cunning and various, sharp here and sickening there, burning here and clawing there. He clutched himself as he hit the ground. The ball squirted away. His breath went away like the ball—a terrible stillness pervaded him—and then, at the onset of panic, his breath came back again. His lips sprayed wetness and he was grateful for the sweet cool air that filled his lungs. But when he tried to get up, his body mutinied against movement. He decided the hell with it. He'd go to sleep right here, right out on the fifty yard line, the hell with trying out for the team, screw everything, he was going to sleep, he didn't care anymore . . .

"Renault!"

The coach's voice scraped like sandpaper against his ears. He opened his eyes flutteringly. "I'm all right," he said to no one in particular, or to his father maybe. Or the coach. He was unwilling to abandon this lovely lassitude but he had to, of course. He was sorry to leave the earth, and he was vaguely curious about how he was going to get up, with both legs smashed and his skull battered in. He was astonished to find himself on his feet, intact, bobbing like one of those toy novelties dangling from car windows, but erect.

Cormier, Robert. 1974. *The Chocolate War.* New York: Dell Publishing, 7–8.

each group take a turn acting out a different word. Be sure to inform them that they will have to perform as a group. Otherwise, each group will elect its own class clown. Given the gift of physical comedy, that kid will immediately know what to do and will need no practice. The result is that the entire group will not be acting but sitting around. To alleviate performance anxiety, brainstorm some different ways groups can prepare their ensemble "performance." These are some typical ideas:

- One person at a time acts out the verb.

- The whole group performs the action at the same time.

- Relay: One person acts while the rest of the members stay frozen until the acting member touches another person. That person comes to life while the original acting member freezes.

In the end you want the students to conclude that well-chosen verbs create a very specific picture that helps tell a better story.

Once students are clear on the characteristics of a vivid verb, their job is to be alert for them as they read their literature circle books. When kids come to the next meeting, part of their preparation should be to mark two or three verbs with sticky notes. Also, they should be able to define the word to the other members, so remind them to ask if they have any questions about the definition, or break down and use the dictionary.

When the book clubs meet, one of their jobs is to notice the words the members marked and start keeping a list of strong verbs in their journals, with the goal of looking back at those words and trying to use them in their own writing. The kids are essentially creating a reader's personal thesaurus. If you combine the lists from all the groups, you'll have a very useful chart that students can refer to when they want to liven up their own writing. The figure shows the master list Nancy's class compiled after two rounds of lit circles.

Working the Room

As students explore how to act out their verbs, first make sure that they are off their duffs and on their feet. Encourage them to really exaggerate their gestures and movements. Tell them that a bit of pantomime is okay if they need to create more of a context for their word.

Later, during lit circle discussions, be sure members don't just point out a chosen word but read the word in a passage so that students can examine it contextually. "Why was this a good word choice?" and "What kind of picture does this word create?" are two questions that should be discussed anytime words are being examined.

Verb Chart

Accentuate	Engulf	Jut	Smack
Babble	Escort	Lurk	Sneer
Bellow	Exasperate	Mesmerize	Spark
Beseech	Excavate	Mingle	Spew
Bide	Flail	Mock	Spring
Blab	Flicker	Muffle	Squabble
Blast	Forge	Perplex	Squint
Bombard	Garner	Pilfer	Squirm
Bristle	Gleam	Ponder	Stalk
Burst	Glimpse	Postulate	Sting
Chirp	Glisten	Premonition	Stride
Clench	Gnash	Prod	Strum
Clobber	Goggle	Pulse	Subside
Clutch	Grapple	Putter	Succumb
Collar	Grimace	Ravage	Surge
Compel	Grovel	Resurrect	Surmise
Conceal	Harpoon	Scatter	Swarm
Conceive	Haunt	Scoff	Tantalize
Conjure	Hiss	Scrutinize	Thrash
Corral	Hobble	Scurry	Throb
Cringe	Hound	Seethe	Traipse
Dart	Hurl	Sever	Trudge
Dash	Immobilize	Shiver	Twinkle
Demolish	Impale	Shudder	Vow
Dictate	Infiltrate	Shun	Worship
Disintegrate	Interrogate	Sidle	Wrench
Distend	Intervene	Skewer	Writhe
Divert	Inundate	Slam	
Drawl	Irk	Slouch	

Reflecting

If time permits after literature circle discussions, it is fun for groups to introduce one or two words by acting them out for the rest of the class.

What Can Go Wrong?

There are always a couple of kids who will just pick any verb rather than hunt for vivid ones. Encourage students to look for verbs that are not already a part of their speaking and writing vocabulary.

The worst thing that can happen is collecting some great lists of verbs—and then just forgetting about them after the book is finished. It's really important to prod the kids to use those lists every time they have to write and whenever you have a few extra moments in class. The more students look at those words and try to use them, the more likely that they will find a home in someone's permanent vocabulary.

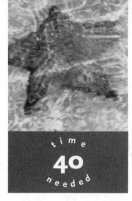

Examining the Setting with Research

Why Do It?

Students need to understand that most books do not take place in their hometown or in times contemporary to their own. Sooner or later all readers have trouble connecting with a novel because their own life experiences have not built the schema necessary to create the full meaning of the text. This is a natural and predictable experience of adventurous readers, so it's important that students have strategies for coping with unfamiliar text details. As kids read, they need to recognize the time period, setting, and historical details that need further research so that their understanding of the book can deepen. Actively pursuing additional background knowledge can make a book more enjoyable and multiply the avenues of conversation when literature circles meet. Also, the more students learn to search for interesting topics and then explore them on the Internet, the better their research techniques will get. When it comes time to write those obligatory research papers, students will already have lots of experiences developing topics, finding good articles that answer important questions, and reading articles in an interactive way.

Teaching the Lesson

Getting Started

It's best to model this activity for the entire class before sending them off on their own research expeditions. That way students are far more likely to find useful information when they hit the Internet.

A good way to begin is with a picture book that deals with a different culture or historical period removed from your students' experiences. *Hiroshima No Pika* by Toshi Maruki is a good example. It portrays a young girl's life on the morning of August 6, 1945. Before reading the book aloud, ask students to open their journals: "As I read this story, I want you to listen carefully and jot down questions you have or topics that are unfamiliar." Ahead of time, brainstorm your own topic list, predicting what ideas students may offer. Then, pick one that seems to have high interest value and make copies of a related nonfiction article that deals with the topic. This article can be from any source—a magazine, encyclopedia, textbook, the Internet. Be sure to have the article copies ready on the day you read the story.

After you read the passage, the class works together to create a list of possible topics to research.

After students create a list, discreetly direct them toward the topic for which you've already run off an article. Then have them brainstorm what they know about this topic. Next, pass out an article on the topic (the one that you cleverly prepared in advance). Have the students read it, jotting down connections to the story and noting where they were right or wrong in their original guesses. Finally, reread a part of the story aloud and have the students reflect on how the new information changes their understanding and visualization of the scene.

An important follow-up assignment is for students to pick one of the listed topics to research on their own. Have the kids bring in the articles they find; the information will spur further discussion and you can see what they're able to find on their own. Sometimes kids will bring in pretty useless information. If this happens, it's probably worth the time to take students to the media center for a period or two to hone their research skills.

Where is Hiroshima?

What are Hiroshima's seven rivers?

What was Hiroshima like before it was bombed?

Why did the U.S. make Hiroshima a target?

What were air-raids? What did people do?

B-29 planes

Enola Gay

Why was the bomb named "Little Boy"?

How does an atomic bomb change the weather?

What was left after the bombing?

How were victims treated medically?

Radiation Contamination

Radiation Sickness

Hiroshima Survivors

This teacher-led activity works perfectly with required, whole-class books, which are often chosen for their superb ability to transport the reader to other times and places. For example, early in *To Kill a Mockingbird* Jem loses his pants on the back fence of the Radleys' collards patch. Many students from areas outside the South have never eaten collards, let alone seen what the plant looks like. Introducing some background information enables students to picture that scene more fully. Much later in the novel, Tom Robinson is shot while trying to escape from prison. Typically students say, "But

World War II Artillery
Pacific Island Warfare
Nimitz
Coded Messages
Spies
Yamamoto
Bataan Prisoners Of War
Medical Care

Atticus was going to appeal." Reading an article about Mississippi's Parchman State Penitentiary helps students better understand the conditions Tom faced and his motivation for escape.

Once students understand the tremendous difference background knowledge can make in understanding and appreciating a novel, they can consciously bring more of it to their literature circles. At the end of the first meeting, students start making a list of topics, places, or historical events that they would like to know more about. This list is updated at the end of each meeting. In the example above, students were reading the historical novel *The Last Lieutenant* by John J. Gobbell. This book focuses on the Japanese invasion of the Philippines and the fall of Corrigador. Complicating matters is the fact that a Nazi spy has taken on the identity of a dead U.S. cryptologist. If he succeeds in making contact, his information will enable the Japanese to defeat the U.S. at Midway.

After the second or third meeting, students review the list and decide which topics they want to research in more detail. Each member picks a topic of personal interest and commits to finding a useful article to read and report on. Before discussing their research with the group, students should read their articles carefully, jot down notes like the ones modeled earlier, and be ready to explain how the information connects with the novel. The discussion of these articles can be scheduled for a couple of days later or can be included in the next literature circle meeting.

Depending on how long the books are and how much background research is needed, this activity can be used just once or it can become an ongoing part of each literature circle discussion.

This strategy is particularly useful when students are reading historical fiction, since this genre melds an author's imaginative storyline with real-life events. As a reader, it's often difficult to determine where the facts end and the fiction begins. This point was made clear by a group that was reading *The Eye of the Needle* by Ken Follett, a rousing tale of espionage during World War II. As the group read, they began wondering if England did indeed create decoy airfields in the hopes of misleading enemy spies. They also wanted to know how important spies really were during the war. Their research revealed that Follett had done his homework. The use of military decoys was a common ploy used by Britain, and both the Allies and the Axis powers relied heavily on information provided by spies.

Working the Room

As you listen in on the discussions, you may need to actively encourage students to take the next step and make connections between their different articles. Sometimes, after each kid has taken a turn summarizing and explaining, the discussion can grind to a halt unless students understand that their next task is to compare, connect, and chew on all this valuable information.

Reflecting

We like to have students write in their journals about the background information brought in by the various members. Specifically, we want students to reflect on what they understand better about the book, thanks to the research material provided by the group members. If time permits, have a few groups

Discusssion of _Wolf by the Ears_ by Anne Rinaldi

> We had a really interesting discussion about Thomas Jefferson's relationship with Sally Hemings. A couple of us wanted to find out if Harriet was a real person or just made up. We found out that Harriet was a daughter of Sally but probably her father wasn't Thomas Jefferson. When they did DNA tests on ancestors of the Hemings family, the tests showed that only Eston, Sally's youngest child, might have been fathered by Jefferson. When we compared articles, we found that different websites present the information different ways. The Monticello website said that at the time Sally became pregnant with Eston, there were 25 different male Jeffersons that carried the DNA that would have matched the test, so the tests really don't confirm whether Jefferson was the father or not. The Sally Hemings site I found said that Thomas Jefferson was definitely the father of Eston. It's interesting that the official Jefferson site tries to ignore his relationship with Sally Hemings.

share a bit about their novel, the topics that arose, and what interesting information they found.

What Can Go Wrong?

As mentioned earlier, sometimes students will bring in low-quality information, so it's a good idea to make the research articles due a couple of days before the actual discussion. Plan to give the kids some time in class to read and jot notes. That way you can catch the weak articles and make sure that the material has been carefully read prior to the literature circle meeting.

Students will often print out the first thing they find rather than scroll through a few pages of hits to uncover a truly useful article. If you see kids who've settled for irrelevant or dubious text, talk to them individually and determine the problem. The most common answer will be: "I was in a hurry and printed the first thing I saw." A bit of counseling and cajoling usually elicits improved quality in the next assignment. It may also help to have those

Drought

Migration to California

Depression

Prison

Cars

students return to the example article you presented earlier so they can observe what high-quality research looks like. However, if lots of students are having trouble finding good articles, it's time for a quick mini-lesson on how to determine the best keywords for a search and then comb through the hits for a good article.

Another common research problem is starting with lists that are too vague and broad. The sample list above is based on *The Grapes of Wrath* by John Steinbeck.

You can easily imagine what irrelevant articles might pop up from this group's list. What does the driving test of the 2006 Corvette have to do with Steinbeck's classic? If groups are having this problem, we have them keep a piece of folded loose-leaf paper in the text. It acts as a bookmark but also encourages students to jot down more specific research topics. We tell them, "Whenever you read, have the bookmark out and a pen in hand. Anytime you see an unfamiliar place or historical event, write it down. Be as specific as possible. Try to use the author's exact words."

If you collect the articles after kids' discussions, you may notice that they underlined parts of an article but failed to jot down any corresponding notes.

Emphasize that the notes are actually more important than the underlining because they record what you were actually thinking as you read the article. When this problem arises, the best solution is to repeat the Think-Aloud lesson in Chapter 2 so that students better understand how you want them to think and take notes with their own research.

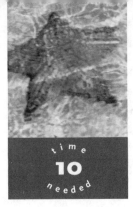

The Envelope, Please: Predicting Plot and Character

Why Do It?

Smart readers are always predicting. They continually speculate on the answers to key questions: What's going to happen to the main characters? How will the plot resolve itself? What motifs that appeared early in a book will grow in importance? And, at a larger level, what is this book trying to be about? What is the theme, message, or purpose that is unfolding as I turn these pages?

Of course, most of us veteran readers do this predicting at an unconscious level. In fact, we only notice how much we have been predicting when a character suddenly does something that makes us say, "Wait a minute! That's not right! She'd never do that!" Our students, however, may not have this prediction predilection built into their cranial hard drives quite yet, and so this lesson shows them how to make predicting very conscious—and to give some thought to character and theme as well.

When book clubs have finished about a third of a book—when the key characters have been introduced and all major conflicts set in motion—it's time for The Envelope, Please. We've based this mini-lesson on a related activity called "line of thought," which we learned from our New York colleague Lucy Calkins (2000).

Teaching the Lesson

Getting Started

Surprise is an important element of this lesson. Start by telling students to put their literature circle books under their desks. Then explain that they are going to predict the endings of their books using The Envelope, Please form (use the one provided in the appendix or one of your own creation). Have students quietly and individually complete the form, recording their best guesses and rationales about the outcomes. You may need to patrol the room to prevent whispered and premature consensus building (quite a compliment to your normally collaborative climate, if you think about it).

Next, have one or two kids share their predictions with the whole class, just for general flavor. This won't be scintillating since not everyone is reading the same book. If kids want to change their predictions based on what these students say, they can amend their forms, but shouldn't scratch out their original predictions. Who knows? Their first instincts may turn out to be right.

Working the Room

Now send the kids off to their regular book club meetings with this instruction:

> Start your meeting by comparing your predictions about the rest of the book. Make sure everyone has a chance to share their ideas. Ask each other questions, debate the different views, and use the book (only the part you've read so far—no cheating!) to see if the ideas are defensible. Your goal is to come up with a group prediction about the fate of one character and resolution of the plot.

Give each group one extra copy of the prediction form for their group forecasts. While students share and debate each other's predictions, circulate to make sure they share airtime equitably and cover both character and plot.

At debriefing time, distribute blank envelopes with a flourish, and have students seal both their individual and group predictions away until the last book club meeting. On the front of the envelope goes the title of the book, the names of the students, and the date. We like to have kids put their signatures along the back flap, just like a confidential recommendation letter, and then the envelopes are stashed in the teacher's desk.

Reflection

The final step comes several days or weeks later, when books are completed. On the final day of discussion, distribute the envelopes to the groups and invite them to unseal their predictions. There may be a few hoots of triumph as prescient kids congratulate themselves on their good guesses, and groans as wrong predictions are revealed. While kids will, of course, remember some of their predictions, the little shades of difference sometimes take on huge proportions at this juncture: "I told you that dog was gonna die!" The important part of the discussion centers around *how* people made successful predictions. Encourage kids to ask each other: "What made you think that? How did you see that coming? What were the clues?"

What Can Go Wrong?

When making their predictions from the first third of the book, kids may be tempted to simply flip ahead and see how the story ends. If that's a worry, hand out rubber bands and have kids seal off the back of the book beforehand so they won't be tempted to "cheat" on their predictions. A bigger concern at the early stages of the lesson is when kids latch onto other people's predictions. We want to help students with discrepant or original ideas about a book to have a voice and not get steamrolled by conventional thinking.

Even kids who have read the book before or otherwise know the ending should fill out the individual prediction sheet and explain how specific outcomes develop from the earlier parts of the book, which they may not have consciously thought about. Obviously, they must disqualify themselves while the rest of the group negotiates its predictions, but that doesn't mean these students have to be silent. As long as they can keep a poker face, they can contribute helpful, probing questions (e.g., "What makes you think the family will get back together?") as the group builds consensus.

The Envelope, Please...

Group Name _____

Date _____ Book Title <u>Dances with Wolves</u>

Mark down what page you are on right now <u>117</u> and the total book pages <u>313</u>

Part I—Character

Based on what you've read so far, which character do you think will experience the greatest change by the end of the book? Think about changes in physical circumstances, lifestyle, relationships, or thinking/values. Describe what you think is going to happen to this character by the time the story is over. Briefly describe the clues in the story that make you think this.

> I think Lieutenant Dunbar will change the most. His lifestyle will become more like the Comanche's. Also, his thoughts on Indians is changing.

> Clues: Kicking Bird and the other Indians saw Dunbar as a friendly and funny person. After being alone for so long, Dunbar was glad to be with the Indians.

Part II—In the End

Based on what you've read so far, how do you think the book will end? What problems will be resolved? What will happen to the main characters other than the one you discussed in Part I? Briefly describe the clues in the story that make you think this.

> Stands with a Fist is white but raised by Indians. She is afraid of whites, especially soldiers and I think when Dunbar saved her she may end up learning that not all white soldiers are bad. Also, since Dunbar is becoming friendly with the Indians, he will join the tribe by the end of the book.

> Clues: Dunbar befriends Stands with a Fist. He appreciates the gifts the Indians give him. Two Socks, a wolf, is almost a dog to Dunbar. This shows that he is in touch with nature, just like the Indians.

A blank version of this form can be found in the appendix.

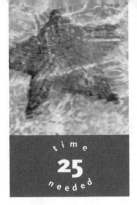

time
25
needed

Looking at Characterization

Why Do It?

When reading a novel, the biggest turn-on (or turn-off) is the characters. If an author creates vibrant characters, we'll want to finish the book. The characters don't necessarily have to be people we want to be best friends with, but they at least need to be genuine, surprising, or captivating. Since characterization plays such an integral role in the reader's experience, how the author crafts the characters is a valuable topic for literature circle groups to explore.

Teaching the Lesson

Getting Started

Have students turn to the next blank page in their journals and describe how an author creates a character. Let students write for a few minutes and then take some responses from volunteers. The next figure shows some typical comments.

From this quick discussion, students will begin to recognize that characterization is revealed in three basic ways: through the author's narration, through the comments and thoughts of other characters, and through what the character says and does.

Next, read aloud a short yet strong example that demonstrates each of these characterization techniques. Following are three that we especially like.

How they look
The way they talk — slang, accent
The way they walk, eat, do things
What they think
What they say to other characters
What other characters say or think about them
The choices they make
How they get along with other characters

The first example illustrates what the author can reveal about a character through third-person narration. This excerpt is from a young adult novel, *The Silver Kiss*, by Annette Curtis Klause. In this paragraph, the author's narration introduces us to Simon, a main character and a vampire.

Simon wiped the rat's blood from around his mouth. It was not as satisfying as human blood, but it would do. There had been no food in the park, except the girl, of course. She had surprised him. He didn't like surprises. But now he remembered the way she had held him with her eyes, and the slight taste of fear in the night air. He regretted having left so fast.

Second is an example of characterization developed by what one character says about another. This excerpt is from the young adult novel *Martyn Pig*, by Kevin Brooks. Here the main character, Martyn, describes his aunt:

Think of the worst person you know, then double it, and you'll be halfway to Auntie Jean. I can hardly bear to describe her, to tell you the truth. Furious is the first word that comes to mind. Mad, ugly, and furious. An angular woman, cold and hard, with wiry blue hair and a face that makes you shudder. I don't know what color her eyes are, but they look as if they never close. They have about as much warmth as two depthless pools. Her mouth is thin and fire engine red, like something drawn by a disturbed child. And she walks faster than most people run. She moves like a huntress, quick and quiet, honing in on her prey. When I was younger I had nightmares about her. I still do.

The third example shows how the author uses a character's own statements and actions. This excerpt is from the memoir *Rocket Boys*, by Homer H. Hickman, Jr. This scene illustrates the antagonistic relationship between the author and his older brother.

Our last fight . . . began when Jim found my bike lying on top of his in the back yard. My bike's kickstand had collapsed (probably hadn't levered it all the way down) and my bike had fallen on top of his, taking them both down. Furious, he carried my bike to the creek and threw it in. . . . Jim stomped up to my room, where I was reading a book, slammed open the door, and told me what he had done and why. "If anything of yours ever touches anything of mine again," he bellowed, "I'll beat the ever-loving hell out of you!"

"How about right now, fat boy?" I cried, launching myself at him. We fell into the hall, me on the inside punching him in the stomach and him yowling and swinging at the air until we rolled down the stairs and crashed into the foyer, where I managed a lucky hit to his ear with my elbow. Howling, he picked me up and hurled me into the dining room, but I got right up and hit him with one of Mom's prized cherry-wood chairs, breaking off one of its legs. He chased me into the kitchen, whereupon I picked up a metal pot off the stove and bounced it off his noggin. Then I made for the back porch, but he tackled me and we fell through the screen door, ripping it off its hinges. We wrestled in the grass until he got up and then leapt back on top of me. That's when I felt my ribs crack. My ribs felt like they were caved in. Blood flowed from my nose. A knot on Jim's head was rising. . . . We had managed some real damage to each other and knew we'd gone too far at last.

After each passage, ask students what has been revealed about the character and how that affects the reader's feelings. Also, have students consider how reliable the information is. One character might not necessarily be giving completely accurate information about another since that information is always colored by perception, whereas an author's third-person narration is usually impartial.

After examining these examples, students return to their literature circles and in their journals make a list of the major characters in the novel their group is reading. Then each student picks a character to follow, keeping notes on how that character's traits and motivations are revealed.

During the remaining literature circle meetings, students spend a few minutes comparing notes on characters, talking about what they noticed, what makes the characters "tick," and how the characters influence each other's actions. Also, because students often choose passages that contain some question related to character motivation, having members who are "character experts" adds depth to these discussions, since students will be more likely to bring up previous characterization details than they would otherwise.

Working the Room

When students begin to discuss characterization, remind them to always question the reliability of information that comes from another character. Also, how does each character have a unique perspective of the story events?

Reflecting

After a couple of discussions, have students reflect on some questions:

- How has your character changed since the beginning of the novel?
- What strategies has the author used to create the character? Are all three used evenly or do you notice one that stands out?
- Why do you think the author made that decision as she wrote?

Sample Character Chart

Book Title: *North and South*
Character: Ashton Main

Page #	Character Description/Action	Insight/Reaction
81	8 years old, Ashton is much prettier than her younger sister, Brett. Ashton tells her that she'll have a hard time finding a boyfriend when she's older.	This girl is mean and likes hurting her sister's feelings.
82	Ashton steals an egg from a heron's nest. When Brett tries to get her to put it back, she says, "If it isn't mine, it isn't yours either." Then she smashes it.	Violent, jealous, purposely does things to hurt her sister.
360	Ashton doesn't really like Billy Hazard, but because Brett does, she makes a play for him. She's 15 now.	Selfish just to be selfish. Brett has never been mean to her. It's like Ashton constantly wants revenge against her sister but there's no reason.
386	Billy is attracted to Ashton because of her beauty and that she's "easy," but there's something about her that makes him uncomfortable.	Maybe he can sense that the only reason she's interested in him is to get back at Brett. He ends up dumping Ashton for Brett. (408)
427	Ashton starts having sex with Forbes even though he is courting Brett and she is engaged to James Huntoon. Plots with Forbes to get back at Billy and Brett.	Completely untrustworthy, good at lying, knows how to use sex to get what she wants. Family or love mean nothing to her.
483	When Ashton visits West Point, she sneaks off and has sex with seven different cadets in one night. She keeps a fly button from each as a souvenir.	Doesn't she worry about getting pregnant or catching something? She's engaged! She is such a slut.

Page #	Character Description/Action	Insight/Reaction
504	After Ashton's return home, she's pregnant. Taking a big risk, Madeleine helps her to get an abortion.	All Ashton does is complain. She never thanks Madeleine or tries to help her when she needs it. Ashton doesn't deserve anybody's help; why do people give it to her?
513	Ashton marries James Huntoon even though she doesn't love him at all, but he has money and is a respected lawyer. She continues her affair with Forbes.	Ashton's beauty and manipulation must just blind guys, but Billy was able to see through it. Ashton is greedy.
760	When Brett and Billy get married, Ashton plots an ambush with Forbes. She wants Billy dead. Orry disowns her from the family.	Ashton is way beyond jealous. She's crazy. People don't mean anything to her. The only important person is herself. I'm glad Orry kicked her out!

What Can Go Wrong?

Less-motivated students may try to pick characters that will be easy to monitor, like those who make infrequent appearances or (better yet) die early in the story. So, be on the lookout as groups choose their characters. If a student picks a minor character, give her the choice of following *several* minor characters or trading the minor character for one more integral to the story. If a student picks a dead character, this is what you can say:

Now, I've got to warn you; this character doesn't last through the whole novel. I'm not going to tell you what happens. You'll have to read to find that out. However, once your character is history, you're going to have to pick a new character to follow, so it might be easier in

Character Study Reflection

In the beginning of the book Ashton is just a really pretty little girl. Sure, she hassles her younger sister and is mean to her sometimes, but that happens in any family. It's a little weird how she's kind of hitting on George when he's so much older than she is. But when Ashton hits her teen years, she gets wild and mean. When Billy breaks up with her and starts dating her sister, she really gets pissed off, which I don't even understand since she didn't like Billy that much anyway and ends up having sex with lots of guys, even later when she's engaged! By the end of the story, Ashton tries to have Brett and Billy killed just as they're leaving for their honeymoon. I couldn't believe it!

I think the author uses all three methods of characterization since other characters sometimes think about how mean and unpredictable Ashton is. The author writes about Ashton's beauty and also tells us what she is thinking. That's how I knew way ahead of time that she was going to try to get back at Brett for stealing Billy from her. I think Ashton's character is mostly revealed by her actions. The stuff she does is so mean. I don't know how anyone could hold a grudge like that. I mean, trying to kill your own sister?

---

the long run if you just choose a character who lasts until the final page. But that's your decision.

Variations

A fun activity for the final literature circle discussion is for students to fill out character resumés and then share them with the rest of the group. Of course, each member has to be imaginative and creative, not just repeat information from the novel. At the same time, all of the invented information must fit logically with that character, so members should have sound reasoning behind each of their entries. If you choose to have students follow characters again in a later literature circle, have the groups contribute different questions for a new resumé.

Character Resumé

Character Name Ashton Main | Huntoon

Book Title North and South

The person I most admire is: Myself, I know how to get what I want.

My favorite television program is: "Sex and the City," I like the way those girls deal with guys on their own terms.

One thing I do very well is: Profit from other people's sorrows or failures.

If I had $100: I'd spend it on clothes that show off my great body.

My favorite subject in school was: Business, because I have an eye for making a profit.

Something I really want is: A man who is good looking, wealthy, powerful and good in bed!

Sometimes I worry about: Growing old and losing my good looks.

An important goal for me is: To get my own way 100% of the time.

A blank version of this form can be found in the appendix.

Assessment and Accountability

We live in an age of accountability and assessment—sometimes teachers feel trapped in a frenzy of blame and buck-passing. People who have never set foot in our classrooms keep asking us, sometimes forcing us, to measure, grade, rate, score, track, monitor, judge, evaluate, and record every single behavior of every single student every day. It eats up time, distorts the curriculum, and makes us crazy. We do stuff we wouldn't otherwise do, because someone else is going to test it. Tests, tests, tests. The Italians have a great word for impossible situations like this: *Basta!* Enough!

Sorry, we just had to vent.

And then we think about adult reading groups, those regular gatherings of lifelong readers that are the model for our classroom clubs. What kind of accountability and assessment happen there? Typical adult book clubs do not formally assess their members, of course. In fact, they usually tolerate a very wide range of "achievement." If some people are quiet and don't talk a lot, they don't flunk the state assessment in the spring; if others come without reading the book, they aren't "held back" to repeat the book club next year. And whoever is hosting the monthly meeting certainly doesn't hand out grades as people go out the door.

But there *is* some natural and appropriate accountability, even in casual adult groups. Poor performance in certain areas will evoke, not a low grade, but some feedback or intervention by one or more members. See what happens if a participant consistently violates these standards:

Show up on time.

Read the book.

Listen actively.

Contribute ideas.

Share airtime.

Respect others' ideas.

Stick to the book.

Back up your opinions.

It may take awhile, and the process may be awkward, but most book clubs will eventually act to enforce these standards.

It is this kind of accountability to oneself and to the group that we stress in this chapter's mini-lessons. We offer tools that help students

- reflect upon their own performance as a group member and set achievable goals for future improvement
- use their classmates as mirrors that can help them grow
- use classroom technology to enhance self-analysis
- become researchers of group process and literary conversation

We include a final mini-lesson on giving grades for book clubs, our cheerful and practical nod to reality. Many of us work in schools or districts where grades are required for any classroom activity lasting more than a few minutes. And until that changes (perhaps by patient teacher action), we have to comply.

The good news: We can assess kids' performance in literature circles in a variety of valid ways without undermining the delicate, personal nature of the groups we are creating. Actually, we have written quite a lot about assessment tools in our other books (Daniels 2001; Steineke 2002). Here we offer our favorite one: making a grading rubric with students. This mini-lesson not only leads to valid, defensible grades for curious administrators and parents, but also engages students in deep discussions about what good reading, thinking, and talking look like. Designing performance assessment rubrics with students is one of those exceedingly rare instances where assessment actually does support instruction.

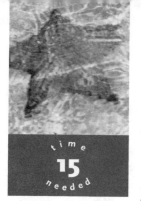

Post-Discussion Journaling

Why Do It?

The laws of physics make it impossible for one teacher to listen in on seven or eight different conversations at once. But we teachers really want to know what's going on. A good surrogate way to assess the quality of book club meetings is to have students write about a discussion highlight, describing in some detail what was said about one specific topic. To get the students to buy into this writing assignment, this is what we emphasize:

> *Really paying attention to the ideas of others and working to remember what was said in a discussion makes you a more attentive listener and helps you understand the book better. Also, recalling your own contributions helps you improve your end of the conversation in upcoming meetings.*

Teaching the Lesson

Getting Started

Tell students that they are to listen extra carefully to what each person has to say and actively pursue their discussion topics in depth rather than jumping from topic to topic without getting everyone's input. Before sending kids to the groups, give them a few minutes of solo time to prioritize their notes, starring the ones that seem to have the greatest discussion potential. Once the groups have gathered, remind the class that discussion can be extended by remembering to Save the Last Word for Me and by asking lots of follow-up questions. Then preview the next step: "It's important to pay close attention to what your members have to say because after this discussion you'll be writing about the best idea that was discussed."

After discussion, either have students open to a fresh page in their journals or pass out eight-by-five-inch index cards. Instruct students to think about the meeting their group just had and pick one topic that sparked an interesting and prolonged discussion. The starter for this discussion could have been a passage, question, connection, or illustration. Once they've thought of the specific "discussion highlight," they should describe the discussion in as much detail as they can, noting the ideas various members came up with as well as any follow-up questions that were asked.

Students will have a much better idea of what you want if you show them a couple of examples, preferably from books they are familiar with but not ones that groups are currently reading. The figure shows a discussion highlight from a group that was reading *Fail-Safe*, by Eugene Burdick.

Student Discussion Highlight from *Fail-Safe*

A discussion topic I brought up centered on the conversations taking place in the plane cockpit of Lieutenant Colonel Grady, the leader of Squadron 6. I asked, "What emotions do you believe were felt by the crew in the cockpit when the fail-safe box went off?" I started the discussion by offering my opinion. I felt that Grady and his crew were overwhelmed with a sense of disbelief. They were trained that the fail-safe box and the technology that controlled it could never make a mistake. Laura and Megan agreed and also felt that the emotions of confusion and fear were going through their minds. Anthony and Tony were curious how the crew felt, knowing that their country could be at war at that very moment. In addition, we all felt there was some sadness in the cockpit, but each airman had to mask his emotions and complete the mission, dropping a nuclear bomb on Moscow.

Working the Room

The writing is best completed immediately after the discussion while memories are fresh. Looking over kids' shoulders as they jot down their discussion highlights can give you some insight into group functioning. The brevity or depth of a discussion highlight is a pretty good barometer of how well a group is using the various discussion skills. If a student focuses mainly on his own opinions and neglects to mention what his members thought, that's a sign his group may need a refresher lesson on Save the Last Word as well as a discussion of what good listening and sharing look like. Your study of the highlight notes will suggest how to "work the room" most efficiently during the next discussion.

Understanding what students view as discussion highlights gives you a real insight into how young readers react to various texts. Sometimes the reader responses are truly surprising, because kids will see things that never would have occurred to you. For instance, see the next example from a quite unusual discussion of *The Grapes of Wrath* by John Steinbeck.

Reflecting

After students finish their discussion highlights, have them look back at what they wrote and brainstorm more ways to deepen their discussions. Sometimes this means reviewing Save the Last Word for Me or reminding themselves how to ask follow-up questions. This is also a good time to discuss what kinds of questions or passages really get a discussion rolling and then develop a list of common characteristics.

What Can Go Wrong?

The main thing to look for in a discussion highlight is a variety of ideas and details. An overly general description indicates one of three things:

- The group is having some trouble sustaining an in-depth discussion.

- The member was not prepared.

- The writer needs to see another written example of a good discussion highlight.

Student Discussion Highlight from *The Grapes of Wrath*

> During our first discussion, I had a passage that had to do with when Tom Joad got to his family's house. When he got there, they were gone and the gate was open. I said that his mother always kept the gate closed because one time the pig got out, and went over to the neighbor's house and ate the baby. We were all trying to imagine the pig eating the baby. We thought it would be kind of funny just seeing the pig, and it's got an arm hanging out of its mouth. We were also trying to figure out if it would be a kind of cannibalism when the family killed the pig and ate it. It was an interesting and fun conversation to have.

A group that's having trouble should be monitored more closely during the next literature circle meeting to determine the problem. Once diagnosed, intervention might mean a skill mini-lesson just for that group or a private conversation with the individual who is not coming prepared. The next figure is an example of a discussion highlight that would raise a red flag.

What's Next

Having students write discussion highlights regularly gives them a record of what worked best in each discussion. Those highlights can also provide fodder for a more formal paper about the book once the lit circle has ended.

Inadequate Discussion Highlight

> The best discussion I led was started by my illustration. The illustration really had a lot of detail. People said it was a great illustration. We also used STLW (Save the Last Word). Everyone guessed what the picture was from the book. I asked the group what preceded the family's move and their thoughts on the picture.

Goal Setting for Group Improvement

Why Do It?

For students to improve their book club discussions, they need to reflect regularly on the quality of their conversations and think of specific ways to improve the next ones. Individual students also need to set goals for improving their reading, their notes, and their own participation.

Teaching the Lesson

Getting Started

At the end of a literature circle meeting, groups should always take a few minutes to jot down some of the successes the group saw that day. These might include ways they dug deep into the text, the growth of specific discussion skills, or actions that helped the group get along better and enjoy each other's company.

Once groups have recognized their positives, they should also identify something that would result in a better discussion next time. We usually ask, "What is one thing your group needs to do differently at the next meeting so that your discussion improves?"

Setting a general goal isn't enough. The group also needs to come up with a plan, listing at least three specific things members are going to say or do that will help the group carry out its goal.

Three Successes

1. Everyone came prepared
2. We remembered to call on Mike first rather than last
3. We complimented each other's good ideas or questions

Improvement Goal: Remember to Save The Last Word For Me when we show our illustrations.

Improvement Goal Plan

1. Assign someone to remind others to wait if they start to explain something right away
2. Hold the picture up for at least five seconds so that everyone has enough time to think of something to say
3. Write SAVE THE LAST WORD FOR ME in big letters on the back side of the illustration to remind the artist to let others explain the picture first

Working the Room

Some groups will tell you that they have nothing to improve. If that happens, offer these suggestions:

- *What skills do you actively use in your discussion? Which one do you use the least? Using that skill more can be your goal.*

- *If you're short on ideas, I can tell you goals that other groups have found helpful. Would you like to hear them or do you think you can come up with something on your own?*

- *If you're good at all the skills we've been working on, then it's time to start working on a new one. Go back and look at the list of discussion skills that's in your journal and pick a new one that would most influence your group's success. Work out a T-chart for it and that will be your goal plan.*

Reflecting

It's important for groups to state their goals and plans to the entire class. Public declaration increases commitment. Plus, hearing everyone else's goals gives groups more ideas for their own goal setting. You might even have students keep a master list in their journals of possible improvement goals. That way, if a group gets stuck thinking up a new goal, they can always mine the list for ideas.

What Can Go Wrong?

Unless you tell groups to review their previous goals at the beginning of the next meeting, they will probably forget. Setting improvement goals doesn't work unless the plans are reviewed frequently. Then, at the end of the meeting, the group should reflect on how well the goal was met. Kids don't always need brand-new goals for each meeting. Many times it takes several meetings to master an improvement goal. Students should keep revising the plan and brainstorming different ways to meet the goal. The more they think about what they should be saying and doing in specific terms, the more likely the group will finally exhibit the discussion improvement they have set for themselves.

What's Next?

Students can set individual as well as group goals. Instead of having the entire group choose a discussion skill to improve, each member picks a skill that he needs to refine and then lists five new things he can say or do to hone that skill. Sometimes we have students review their reading notes (sticky notes, bookmarks, etc.) and reflect on how useful they were in the discussion. What worked? What fell flat? What can students do differently so that their questions, passages, illustrations, or connections do a better job generating discussion and fresh ideas?

time
20
needed

Using Student Observers

Why Do It?

When you have thirty students meeting in a half dozen book clubs, you can observe and coach each group for only three or four minutes a day—if you're lucky. And that's not enough for groups to grow at top speed. One way to provide more feedback to kids about their discussion skills is to train the students to be their own observers. No, we're not talking about turning one kid into a little cop who rats out the evil-doers to the teacher. Believe it or not, kids can assess each other accurately if you set up a dispassionate and fair mechanism. Using observation sheets is part of the secret, and it's also a good way to emphasize the skills you want the groups to work on.

Teaching the Lesson

Getting Started

Before sending students off to observe and record the discussion skills of their fellow members, it's vital to model this strategy for the entire class. Start by having the students read a very short story and take discussion notes.

Next, ask for five volunteers to discuss the story in front of the class. Before this group sets up, pass the observation sheets to the rest of the class. (See the appendix for a blank master of this form.) On the overhead show them where to put the names of those being observed, how to record the skills being observed by using tic marks, and why quoting members is so important. We start with a blank observation sheet so that observers fill in the

Filled-Out Observation Sheet

Observation Sheet   Name Giana

Book Title To Kill A Mockingbird   Date 3/27/01 Hour 1

Skills	Group Members				Total
	Gina	Sam	Andy	Tori	
Support and Friendliness	LHT LHT	LHT LHT	LHT LHT	LHT	35
Citing Passages	LHT	III	III	III	14
Discussion Starters	LHT II	III	IIII	II	16
Follow-up Questions	III	LHT I	LHT	II	16
Encouraging Participation-Getting opinions	LHT I	LHT II	III	IIII	20
Total	31	29	25	16	

Notes: Write down some specific things each member said that showed they were using one of the observed skills.

GOAL: Encouraging Participation/Getting opinions

"Nice question Gina"
"Keep going Sam."
"Do you have anymore questions from this chapter?"
"I liked that passage Tori."
"Come on Andy let's hear your opinion."
"Tori, you go next."

A blank version of this form can be found in the appendix.

initial information correctly. Then we show students a completed observation sheet from a previous class.

When the volunteer group prepares for the discussion, assign one of the five to act as an observer as well, but have the group observer record on an observation sheet transparency rather than paper. Make sure the group observer has nothing on her desk except the observation sheet. Then sit down with the rest of the class and let the demonstration group proceed with about ten minutes of discussion. At the end of that time, thank the group and let them return to their seats.

Have the class tally the results from their individual observations. Adding the numbers across each row determines how many times the group used a skill; adding the numbers in each column shows how many times each person in the group participated while using the observed skills. First ask, "What conclusions about how the group worked together can you draw by looking at the tic marks?" Students will notice that certain members used some skills more than others, or that one member got a ton of tic marks while another person had hardly any. Then ask, "From the data on the observation sheet, what are some discussion goals this group could set for next time?" Responses might include these suggestions:

- Have the person who talked the most always answer last.

- Try to use the least-used skill more often.

- Have the person who talked the most be the observer next time to see how the discussion changes.

- Create a new T-chart for the least-used skill and then keep it out for the next discussion.

Next we compare the results between the different observers. When numbers vary widely (e.g., one student records twelve follow-up questions while another counts thirty-three), we discuss what could have accounted for the difference in perception. It might turn out that one student recorded all questions while the other one didn't count lead questions or yes/no follow-ups. What we try to emphasize is that as an observer you have to be clear on how you are defining a skill and then be consistent in your record keeping.

Also, be sure to compare the class's tallies with those of the group observer. Often those numbers will vary noticeably. That's because a group's observer often gets caught up listening to the conversation and forgets to write anything down. Students need to be consciously aware of this pitfall whenever they observe.

Working the Room

During the demonstration discussion, you should act as an observer, too. All eyes and focus should be on the discussion group.

Reflecting

After the practice observation, ask the students whether they found observing easy or difficult. Students often notice that for a while they forgot to observe because they became focused on the content of the conversation. Many will comment on how hard it is to keep up; while they're trying to decide where to record a comment, the discussion keeps moving forward. It's important for students to know that they'll never catch everything, but they need to be as accurate as possible with what they do record.

What Can Go Wrong?

The biggest problem with using observation sheets during actual discussions is that the groups sometimes fake it. They'll tell the observer to just mark skills so that it looks like they're doing what they're supposed to. The best way to prevent this is to conduct (or repeat) the demonstration lesson before turning the groups loose with the observation sheets. Also, having ongoing conversations about the observation sheets can improve the quality. When you see some good or poor examples, hide the names and make a transparency; then reflect on how useful this observation sheet would be for improving discussion.

What's Next?

Once observation sheets have been introduced, a good goal is to use them in a series of literature circle discussions so each member can take a turn as observer. Though the observer is not a direct participant in the discussion, don't

Using quiet voices
directing the group's work
describing personal feelings/reactions
    to the work
paraphrasing
Using the text to support an idea
being friendly and supportive
recognizing good ideas
energizing the group
disagreeing with ideas respectfully
asking follow-up questions
using names
answering questions

worry about the observer failing to learn. Not only do observers absorb quite a few of the literary ideas discussed, but keeping track of the discussion details makes the observer much more aware of the various skills and how they influence the quality of the discussion. Once a student has been an observer, she returns to the group as a stronger member because of that heightened awareness.

When students use observers in sequential discussions, we often make photocopies of their observation sheets for each member so that the groups can put them side by side and study the sheets for skill improvements and further goal setting. As students get more adept in the use of observation sheets, we let groups decide which skills they want to observe. The figure above is a list of observable skills that one class brainstormed.

Eye in the Sky Videotaping

time **15** *needed*

Why Do It?

We all agree that students need to become more reflective, to step back and appraise their own efforts in all kinds of school activities, including peer-led book discussions. Reports from outside observers (like teachers) are not enough to help groups see themselves. This mini-lesson, which we picked up from Kathy La Luz at Washington Irving School in Chicago shows kids how to videotape a meeting of their book clubs. Then, at their next meeting, the group reviews the tape and produces a written report reflecting on their performance. This lesson presents kids with two challenges: learning how to look at their own behavior thoughtfully and honestly, and making a technically usable recording.

To introduce this lesson, you need a videotape of a real book club meeting, one that shows both strengths and weaknesses that can be discussed. Ideally, of course, you'll have one from a previous year, with permission from the student "stars" to use the tape in future classes. If you don't already have a tape, gather some colleagues and tape yourselves having a teachers' book club discussion that displays some positive and negative behaviors. Or, get a copy of the video *Strategy Instruction in Action* by Stephanie Harvey and Anne Goudvis (2001), which has an excellent segment of younger kids talking about the novel *Because of Winn-Dixie.*

Teaching the Lesson

....

Getting Started

Here's how you might introduce the lesson:

> *Today we are adding something new. We're going to begin videotaping one literature circle group every day that we have meetings. When it is your group's turn, you'll set up the camera and tape your meeting. Then later, you'll review the tape to see how well your book club is doing. In a few minutes, I'll show you how to set up the camera and get good sound. But first, we need to talk about what we are looking for in these tapes, and how you can use them to make your meetings more fun and effective.*

Hand out the Video Reflections sheet provided in the appendix (or a similar one that reflects the reading and discussion strategies that you stress). Give students a minute to look over the form and ask any questions about it. Now, play five or ten minutes of the tape, that segment you preselected for its assortment of strengths and weaknesses. Then stop the tape and have students write some responses, using the forms. Next, if you have time, allow kids to talk over their assessments in small groups; otherwise move directly to a whole-class discussion. Invite a sharing of responses, question by question: "What strengths did you notice? What could this group do better? If you were a member of the group, what steps could you take to have a better meeting next time?"

Then you can say:

> *This is what you guys are going to be doing. Every day, one group will tape themselves. Then at the next book club meeting, instead of having your regular discussion, you'll play back the tape and talk about your own performance. You'll do it the same way we just did: Write down the strengths you noticed, things to improve, and specific plans. You'll fill out one of these forms as a group and give it to me.*

The last task for the day is to create a schedule for group videotapings. You can assign dates randomly or let groups pick their dates. If they start haggling, you might say: "Since every group is going to get taped eventually, the specific day you get really doesn't matter. But one group has to agree to be videotaped today—right now, as a matter of fact."

Working the Room

Once kids go off to their meetings, you'll need to stick with the group that's being taped, especially when this process is new. The first few times, you'll probably be wrestling with the technology and making sure everyone can be seen and heard. But after a while, the kids should take over the basic tasks of positioning the camera, marking and inserting a blank tape, and initiating the discussion. Once the taping becomes routine, you can go back to visiting book clubs as they meet. In fact, when our friend Kathy uses the "eye in the sky" in her classroom, the group being videotaped is often the only one she *doesn't* visit. Why not? Because she knows it's on tape.

Reflecting

When the students regroup for class sharing time, ask the group that was taping to talk about their experience. With their permission, you could show the first three to five minutes of the meeting. Ask the group members (not the rest of the class; it's premature for outside criticism) to offer some initial impressions. This gives everyone a clear and immediate sense of what their tape is going to look like when their turn comes up.

At the next book club meeting, you'll need to set up equipment so this "pioneer" group can review its tape. That means setting up a VCR and monitor to provide good viewing for the taped group but not a distraction to everyone else, who will be in regular book club meetings. The group obviously cannot watch their entire previous meeting, or they will run out of time. Kids can select a ten- or fifteen-minute section to review, or they can skip ahead a few times and get several samples.

While watching the tape, each member should jot notes on a blank assessment form concerning each category: strengths, weaknesses, and possible changes. After viewing, the group should talk frankly about what worked and what didn't. As a consensus assessment is created, one student records the group's observations on a single form. The real payoff comes when the group members affirm specific steps for improving their next meeting. As a wrap-up, you might stop by the group for the last few minutes to hear a report on their findings and plans.

Weeks later, when all groups have recorded themselves, reviewed their tapes, and submitted assessment forms, you can hold another kind of mini-lesson around questions like these: "What have you learned about your groups from this process? What has changed as a result of watching your-selves at work?"

What Can Go Wrong?

This activity can have a lot of bugs. We'll address the technical stuff first. You have to arrange the seating so that everyone is visible to the camera; usually a tight half-circle works best. It helps if you have a tall tripod so you can crank the camera up high and provide a good look at all the faces. Getting good sound while videotaping in classrooms, especially during small-group activities, can be a challenge. The camera's microphone picks up all the voices and noises in the room; it can't tune in to one part of the noise like the brain-driven human ear can. Thus it's especially important when taping book clubs that all students use their six-inch voices, not their hundred-yard voices.

Finally, when the first group starts taping, it's vital to stop and check the machinery. After two or three minutes, stop the meeting to review the tape for sound level and video, and make adjustments as needed. If the sound is just too jumbled, you'll need to get a plug-in, omnidirectional microphone and place it in the middle of the group. This is not a big-ticket item: Any electronics shack will sell you one for ten bucks.

When the taping process is brand-new, you'll have kids mugging for the camera, acting goofy, hiding their faces, trying to slip "bad" words into the conversation, and every other sort of routine kid behavior. Most of that clears itself up shortly, when kids realize nobody but them will be watching the tape. Getting students to thoughtfully review their own performance in a peer-led group, however, can be awkward at first. It takes some nerve to point out a friend's off-task behavior or to remind someone that he came to the meeting unprepared. And it takes even more courage to say, "Yeah, that was dumb. I did mess up there." Sometimes kids will deal with the social discomfort of the task by submitting an "I'm OK/You're OK" report that doesn't seriously address any shortcomings. If you foresee such situations, sit in on the first few minutes of the viewing and stop the tape frequently to draw kids' attention to both stellar and problem moments.

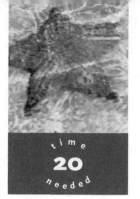

Developing a Rubric with Students

Why Do It?

Teachers often ask us how we grade literature circles. Sometimes they see kids' discussion groups as "too subjective," too fluid, or too personal to allow for traditional A-B-C grading. It certainly is true that evaluating students' performance in a book club discussion is a little tougher than scoring a ten-item factual recall quiz. And it is also true that book clubs, as a collaborative activity, require a level of trust and friendship that can be undermined by competitive grading that pits kids against each other. But literature circles provide a wonderful opportunity to track the growth of kids' reading habits, thinking strategies, and social skills. And we can even award grades, if we absolutely must, that are meaningful, defensible, and student-centered.

This mini-lesson further involves students in self-assessment (already a basic operation in literature circles) and sparks a deep discussion of what effective book club members actually do. The lesson works best as the class approaches the end of a book club cycle, when groups have met several times and are close to finishing their books. Also, this lesson needs to move really briskly: It involves a lot of quick writing, brainstorming, short group meetings, discussion, and consensus building.

Teaching the Lesson

Getting Started

Begin by asking students to write for two minutes on these questions: What do effective book club members do? How do they operate as readers? What kind of ideas do they have? What work habits do they have? How do they behave? What actions do they take in group meetings?

Ask students to list as many traits or characteristics as they can. Then, as volunteers report their ideas, develop a master list on the board or an overhead transparency. Eliminate items that say the same thing ("gives others a turn" = "shares airtime"). Keep stressing that you are looking for the most important and fundamental traits that good book club members have. (You'll probably hear many of the things that you have been teaching kids all along.) When this brainstorming is done, you may have a list of ten or twenty items, far too many for any useful scoring tool.

Next put students into groups (their own book clubs or other combinations) with this instruction: "Look over our list and decide what are the top five most important traits of effective book club members. You may need to combine two or three items on the list or reword a trait we have already listed. Pick someone to be a recorder and be ready to report in five minutes." When groups report back, orchestrate the sharing to create a whole-class consensus list of the top five (or six; it's more important to honor good ideas than choose a certain number). Here's how the discussion sounds in our classrooms:

> Teacher: *Okay, who can share a trait that's very important?*
>
> Student: *Coming prepared to the meetings.*
>
> Teacher: *Coming prepared. Okay. Did any other groups have that on your "Top Five" lists? Every group? Wow. Okay, so that one goes on the list.* (Puts a star beside this entry on the list.) *Now, who had another big one?*
>
> Student: *Taking it back to the book.*
>
> Teacher: *Who else had that one? Five out of six groups. Let's get that one on our list. . . .*

And so on. You gradually shape the consensus-building process until a list of five or six widely recognized traits is agreed upon.

Now comes the fun part—turning the list into a performance assessment rubric. Here's what we say to the kids:

Now we have agreed on six big traits that good book club members have. But are they all equally important? Do some matter more than others? Does "coming prepared" rank just the same as "respecting others' opinions"? I'm giving you 100 points to distribute among the six traits, and three minutes to decide. Be ready to explain why you allocated the points to each item. Back in your groups—go!

When groups return with their scoring, the next step is to create a consensus rubric. You can do this in two ways. One approach is through discussion, like this:

Teacher: *Okay, some group tell us which trait you gave the most points to and how many.*

Student: *We gave 40 points to "proving your ideas with the book."*

Teacher: *Wow, that's a lot. Can you say why?*

Student: *Well, we thought that it's easy to have opinions and talk a lot, but if you can really show people just where in the book your ideas come from, if you can answer people's questions, then you really understand the book.*

Teacher: *All right. How many points did other groups give this item?*

Student: *We gave it 15.*

Teacher: *That's a big difference. Why did you rate it so much lower than those guys?*

You keep on winnowing and negotiating until a thoughtful, reasoned consensus is achieved.

The other approach, quicker but less reflective, is to resolve point differences mathematically, using a chart like the one shown here. Put this up on the board, have one student from each group fill in their section, and then derive a class-average point distribution, keeping inside the 100-point limit. The average may not come out perfectly; but a little creative number-squishing at the last step will create a good-enough outcome.

	Group 1	Group 2	Group 3	Group 4	Group 5
Trait 1					
Trait 2					
Trait 3					
Trait 4					
Trait 5					
Point totals:					
Average:					

Either way, you end up with a student-developed performance assessment rubric you can use for grading students on a cycle of literature circles. The rubric will include several valid criteria, things that effective book club members actually do, and a reasonable weighting of their importance, making it a perfectly appropriate tool for grading. As long as the points add up to 100, you should be able to convert the outcomes to whatever grading scale your school uses.

When it is time to put the rubric form to work, actually grading individual students for their book club performance, you have plenty of options.

- The teacher scores each student, based on observations.

- Each student scores him/herself and submits the assessment to the teacher for approval.

- The teacher and each student fill out forms, then hold a conference to resolve differences.

- The members of each book club fill out a form for each of the other members and:

   1. hand them back to the ratee for private viewing

   2. give them to the teacher as advisory information

   3. have an open discussion in the group about all ratings

- The teacher reviews all self and peer ratings for all students and makes the final decisions.

Obviously, the way you use these rubrics will depend on the trust and maturity level in the classroom. We generally favor openness and discussion; after all, the more kids reflect upon the specific ingredients of success in any activity, the more they are likely to achieve it.

Working the Room

Rove around the classroom during all the student steps in this lesson: while they are jotting individual lists, when groups are meeting to determine the top five traits, and when they divide up the points. This will entail normal checking, prodding, and encouraging. Later, when kids actually use the rubric to grade themselves, you'll also want to be out in the crowd, doing some on-the-fly conferences to make sure kids are being honest and fair to themselves.

Reflecting

This whole mini-lesson is an exercise in reflection on the social process of book clubs and the meaning of thoughtful reading. The only thing left to do, really, is to reflect on the usefulness of the tool itself, after it has been used "for real" to generate a set of grades. When kids receive their book club grade, we ask them to write in their journals for a few minutes, on this prompt:

Is this a fair appraisal of my work in this book club? Have any of my strengths or weaknesses been misrepresented? What goals has this process helped me to set for the next time around? How could we revise the rubric to make it more accurate?"

You can ask for volunteers to share thoughts in a whole-group meeting, have kids hand in their journals for your written response, or tuck these thoughts away until the next cycle of book clubs, when they can be used to revise the rubric.

What Can Go Wrong?

One slightly ironic downside to this student-driven form of assessment is that it can yield pretty low grades. Many rubrics work that way. If you score yourself a couple of points below perfect in five or six traits, you're already down in the B range. So we often find ourselves adjusting kids' scores up.

If you elect to have kids score each other, there are two possible problems:

1. Kids will collude to give each other all A's.

2. Some kids will take the opportunity to slam others.

The best defense against such abuses is to talk about them beforehand. The kids may need to be reminded that you are a very knowledgeable observer, and that implausible ratings will be spotted promptly and dealt with directly.

9
Performance Projects That Rock

As you've probably noticed, we take the notion of modeling student book clubs after adult book clubs rather seriously. So why are we promoting end-of-book projects? Does Oprah have her guests congregate in the crafts corner for a diorama fest after concluding conversation with the author? Of course not. But here's the difference. The people who belong to Oprah's Book Club are already lifelong readers. They're hooked. We're certain that even if Oprah weren't offering book suggestions, these people would still be reading. As a matter of fact, we're willing to bet that they have mental lists of all the books they would like to read if they just had the time. That's where kids are often different. They need a bit more encouragement. If we want them to be lifelong readers, they need to be excited about future reading, always adding to those mental lists.

We devote a lot of energy to selecting great titles for the literature circles and then talking up the choices in order to get the kids excited, so of course our ultimate goal is to interest kids in several books, not just the one their group chose. Sure, some of this cross-pollination will occur via informal teen book chatting. But face it—on their own time, kids will mostly talk to their friends; they won't be actively polling other book clubs for recommendations. So, what are we to do? Have the groups do projects on their books, but make those projects really get the word out.

Performance projects offer a way for students to hone their presentation skills as well as celebrate the conclusion of their literature circle books. Unlike the poster, fake newspaper front page, or diorama, performance projects don't just take up space and gather dust. Though they often take one or two class periods for creation, practice, and performance, the time spent on these projects is well worth it because they are live and interactive. Performance projects require kids to rethink the book in order to create an event that entertains and captivates an audience, most of whom are unfamiliar with the title. When a performance project rocks, it means that a group has just "sold" its book to a new set of readers.

Tableaux

Why Do It?

If you've ever read *You Gotta BE the Book* by Jeff Wilhelm (1997), you already know what a unique and powerful after-reading strategy tableaux can be. For literature circles, this means students take an important passage from their book and turn it into a series of five or six motionless, silent scenes. While one group member reads the text, the others create each scene by freezing in position. This project requires kids to be ruthless in their scripting since the narration is limited to a series of captions. And students must think seriously about the accuracy of their blocking and characterization, which requires them to reread the text carefully. As with the other performance projects in this chapter, tableaux require groups to provide an introduction, so the audience will fully appreciate the scene.

Teaching the Lesson

Getting Started

We like to introduce this strategy by having kids create tableaux scenes using a script from a novel they are already familiar with. The students' job is to create a "freeze frame" that captures the characters, action, and emotion of each scene. Since we want all group members to be actors in at least one or two scenes, the teacher can serve as the narrator for this practice script. Here's an example from *Of Mice and Men.*

Remind students that the most interesting tableaux scenes are created when they remember the following items:

Tableaux Script Example from *Of Mice and Men*

Introduction

Of Mice and Men, written by John Steinbeck and published in 1937, is the story of two men trying to find work during the Great Depression. Though George is Lennie's friend, he also serves as Lennie's guardian because Lennie is mentally handicapped. Though tall and strong, Lennie's behavior is similar to that of a five-year-old. Lennie wants to be a good friend to George but often creates trouble for the two of them because he doesn't understand the consequences of his actions. At the end of the story, Lennie accidentally strangles a woman. Frightened, he then runs away. Although a vicious mob is determined to find Lennie during the manhunt, George finds him first, forcing George to make the most difficult decision of his entire life.

Scene #1—Lennie and George

"Look across the river, Lennie, an' I'll tell you so you can almost see it. We gonna get a little place. We'll have a cow an' we'll have maybe a pig an' chickens . . . an' down the flat we'll have a . . . little piece of alfalfa—"
"For the rabbits," Lennie shouted.

Scene #2—Lennie and George

George raised the gun and steadied it, and he brought the muzzle of it close to the back of Lennie's head. The hand shook violently, but his face set and his hand steadied. He pulled the trigger.

Scene #3—Lennie and George

The crash of the shot rolled up the hills and rolled down again. Lennie jarred, and then settled slowly forward to the sand, and he lay without quivering.

Scene #4—Lennie and George

The brush seemed filled with cries and with the sound of running feet. George sat stiffly on the bank and looked at his right hand that had thrown the gun away.

Scene #5—Lennie, George, Curly

The group burst into the clearing. "You got him, by God. Right in the back of the head."

Scene #6—Lennie, George, Slim

George let himself be helped to his feet.
Slim said, "You hadda, George. I swear you hadda."

- Keep composition tight—actors should be close together.
- Consider the relationships characters have to one another. Characters who are friends or family on good terms will be physically closer to each other.
- Exaggerate the emotional expression your character would be feeling.
- Stagger body heights—it is visually boring when everyone is standing or sitting.

Pass out the scripts and give the groups about ten minutes to practice before performing the scenes. Audience members can best appreciate the scenes if they close their eyes until each scene is frozen in position. Watching the actors set up their positions spoils the effect. That said, we've never been very successful at getting the kids to cover their eyes. Maybe it reminds them of playing Seven-Up in grade school.

After students perform the scenes, we pass out photocopies of the original pages from *Of Mice and Men* (or whatever book the script is from) and have the students compare it to the tableaux script. They should notice that specific lines are chosen for their power. Seldom are all the sentences in a paragraph used for one freeze frame. One paragraph might actually contain

Tableaux from *Of Mice and Men* Script, Scene #5

two or three scenes. Also, lines can be combined from several different paragraphs in order to create a powerful scene caption.

Literature circles then reconvene to script a scene from their own books. Emphasize to the groups that choosing the right scene is very important. A good scene should have action and emotion that can be broken down into about six different freeze frames. Also, given a proper introduction, the audience should be able to understand the plot events even if they haven't read the book.

All members should write a copy of the script as it is negotiated. Remind the groups to keep the freeze frame captions short—when a narrator reads a long paragraph, it's hard to keep standing statue-still.

Once the script is set, the groups need to practice so they can memorize their blocking for each freeze frame. Also, the groups should plan for simple costumes and props (hat, apron, cane, etc.) that will enhance the action and make the different characters clear to the audience.

Working the Room

As in all performance projects, you'll need to prod the kids off their rear ends and demand that they keep practicing and refining their freeze frames. If you can trust them, have groups go out in the hall or to other parts of the building to practice their tableaux. A little surprise factor really enlivens the performance. Watch their blocking and don't be afraid to give suggestions.

Reflecting

Always videotape the tableaux, remembering this key step: Hit the pause button between each freeze frame. That way you eliminate the getting-in-position preliminaries, and the viewers see the scenes the way they would have originally, if they had shut their eyes like you told them.

After viewing the tableaux videotape, the kids should reflect on what worked, what didn't, and what they would do differently to improve the next performance with a new piece of literature.

What Can Go Wrong?

The part that almost always falls flat on the tableaux isn't the blocking; it's the narration. Groups will spend lots of time planning their staging and costumes, but never think twice about coaching the narrator on the oral interpretation of the scenes. So, as you monitor, watch for this problem. When you view the videotape, if the groups' narrators often fail to match the energy of the acting, take time for some direct instruction of basic oral

What Makes a Good Tableaux?

Narration

- Lively, enthusiastic voice
- Speak clearly
- Speak slowly
- Speak loudly
- Show emotion
- Pause between sentences
- Practice lines
- Emphasize key words
- Sound confident, decisive
- Make character voices

Scene Acting

- Audience can see facial expressions from a distance
- Don't laugh—stay in character
- Stand still
- Use props
- Each scene looks different
- Overexaggerate emotions (facial expressions) and gestures
- Audience understands what actors are interpreting
- Blocking shows relationships between characters
- Staggered levels
- Feeling of action or motion
- Creative poses
- Look at audience
- Be dramatic
- Audience can see everyone (no one is behind someone else)

---

interpretation techniques. The nursery rhyme strategy described in the readers theater lesson (the next lesson in this chapter) can be useful here as well.

Variations

Whenever you are doing a whole-class book, the use of tableaux can be an energizing way to review a chapter or discuss reader response. If you give six different groups the same three pages from a novel, each group will script and block differently because every reader's personal picture of the text is unique.

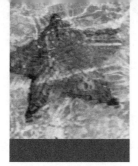

Readers Theater

Why Do It?

Readers theater is a great oral interpretation strategy that groups can use to portray a key scene in a book. Although students must examine the text carefully in order to create an effective script, the performance only requires dramatic reading, so groups don't need to spend a lot of time worrying about costumes, props, blocking, or memorizing.

Teaching the Lesson

Getting Started

The best way to introduce students to readers theater is to have them perform a prepared script from a familiar piece of literature. Draft some students to do a cold reading as the rest of the class follows along. Afterward, have students examine the script and together make a list of the typical readers theater conventions for the presentation of a scene from a novel. Also, have the students compare the original text of the novel with the scripted version. Students should notice the following conventions.

Readers Theater Conventions

- The group must provide an introduction to the book and scene so that the audience understands what is going on.

- Everyone has a part.

- There can be more than one narrator.

- There are choral parts where more than one person reads at the same time.

- The lines and paragraphs are broken up differently for the script.

- It's okay to cut lines from the text when making the script.

- It's okay to add a few choice words to the script.

- Sometimes lines are repeated for emphasis.

Once students understand the conventions, have them look for a two- or three-page scene in their lit circle books that would make a good readers theater production. The kids should look for a scene that has some action or excitement, a strong emotional hook, and a good mix of dialogue and narration.

After choosing the scene, the group needs to come up with an introduction that explains a little bit about the book and how the chosen scene fits into the plot. The introduction should also explain why the group found this scene significant.

Scripting the scene involves breaking up the dialogue and narration into specific parts. First, give each member a photocopy of the chosen pages. Then students go through the text with pencil, marking promising parts and crossing out inappropriate sections. After the preliminary script is negotiated, each member needs to write or type a final version of the script from the draft photocopy. Otherwise, when students present their piece to the class, there will be a lot of stumbling and confusion as they try to read lines with lots of scribbles, cross-outs, and changes.

When students have written out their scripts, the final stage is to practice. Direct students to stand up straight with their feet shoulder-width apart. Otherwise, kids will insist on staying seated while they slouch and mumble their way through the words. During practice, kids should have pencils in hand so they can make notes as they stop and discuss how they should be delivering the lines. Where should they shout? Where should they use a stage whisper? What emotion should a word or line convey? If your kids still read as if they are sleepwalking, make them listen to an old radio show like *The Lone Ranger*. In radio theater, actors had to be expressive because there was no visual element. Those disembodied voices had to carry the reader into an imaginary world. Tell the kids that if they feel like their reading is super corny and hammy, they're doing it right!

The most difficult part of any readers theater piece is making the choral parts "one voice." Tell students to look at the others with whom they are reading in unison. They should assign one person as the leader of these parts. That person uses a slight nod to make sure everyone starts at the same time.

Working the Room

Getting the kids to write their scripts is the easy part. The tough job is working the room when they start practicing those scripts aloud. For some reason, kids do not understand that rehearsing any performance means practicing it as many times as possible, not just once or twice. Unless you patrol the room—maybe even giving points for how many times you witness a group repeating their script from top to bottom—some kids will be sitting around, chatting away about the upcoming weekend. Because they've watched so many movies but never seen all the rehearsals and takes, they assume that acting just comes naturally and needs no forethought. Of course, when they get up in front of the class and choke, it dawns on them that practice would have helped. If you can head off those painful performance moments everyone will be much happier.

As students practice, they will need coaching. Help them with the emotions and oral interpretation. If any kid has the nerve to say this activity is useless because he'll never be an actor, remind that reluctant learner that he's practicing skills that build poise and confidence and make a good first impression—and first impressions count for a lot in a job interview!

Reflecting

Rather than waiting until the final presentation, it's helpful to do some reflection during the process. When groups have finished their scripts and start practicing them, have a short discussion about how people chose particular lines and marked them for interpretation.

Have groups practice in pairs. While one group practices, the other group listens for clarity, vocal variation (versus monotone), and speed. The most common problem students have when they perform is reading too fast.

Finally, be sure to videotape or audiotape the performances. Actually, audiotape is a better choice because the focus of a readers theater project is how the piece is read, not how it looks. Listening to an audiotape, the kids will have to focus on the clarity and dramatic interpretation (or lack thereof) of their reading. Watching a videotape, they'll forget the quality of their oral interpretation and start worrying whether the outfit they wore that day made them look fat or dorky.

What Can Go Wrong?

Some groups will perform readings that could cure an insomniac every time. The key is to direct the debriefing so that those groups acknowledge where they fell short and figure out how they can script or practice differently the next time. Also, if a lot of kids have the "monotone" problem, you probably need to offer some direct instruction on the elements of oral interpretation and have them practice with very short pieces of text. Nursery rhymes work well for this. Taking turns with a partner, have the kids recite the one nursery rhyme they remember, but with an emotional twist: Say it like they're angry, sad, happy, frightened, and so forth. Then ask for volunteers to recite their rhyme to the class, conveying emotion and context. Here are some sample prompts for reciting "Little Miss Muffet":

- Recite as if you are Tony Soprano. Muffet owes you a ton of money from an old gambling debt and refuses to pay up!

- Recite as if you are giving an acceptance speech at the Academy Awards and Muffet is the person to whom you owe everything.

- Recite as if you are Muffet's employer. When she should have been at work, she was sitting on that darn tuffet of hers and you are sick of her unreliability.

- Recite as if you are the spider, gleefully relating the Muffet story to your spider friends.

Readers Theater Script from *The Wonderful Wizard of Oz*

Introduction

The Wonderful Wizard of Oz, written by Frank Baum, was originally published in 1900. In a story that most of us know, thanks to the film starring Judy Garland, Dorothy is whisked away from her home in Kansas to the land of Oz. When asked for his help in returning her to Kansas, the Wizard demands that she first destroy the Wicked Witch. Close to the castle, Dorothy is captured, and the Wicked Witch devises a plan to steal Dorothy's magical silver shoes. In this scene, the witch has managed to trip the girl and grab a silver shoe as it flies off Dorothy's foot. However, the witch's glee turns out to be short-lived.

Narrator #1:	The Wicked Witch was greatly pleased with the success of her trick.
Narrator #2:	For as long as she had one of the shoes, she owned half the power of their charm and Dorothy could not use it against her.
Dorothy:	Give me back my shoe!
Witch:	I will not!
Narrator #1:	Retorted the witch.
Dorothy:	You are a wicked creature! You have no right to take my shoe from me.
Witch:	I shall keep it, just the same, and some day I shall get the other one from you, too.
Narrator #1:	Said the witch, laughing at her.
Narrator #1:	This made Dorothy so very angry
Narrator #2:	That she picked up the bucket of water that stood near and dashed it over the witch,
Both Narrators:	Wetting her from head to foot.
Narrator #1:	Instantly the wicked woman gave a loud cry of fear and then began to shrink and fall away.
Witch:	See what you have done! In a minute I shall melt away.

Narrator #1:	Melt away
Narrator #2:	Melt away
Both Narrators:	Melt away!
Dorothy:	I'm very sorry indeed.
Narrator #2:	Said Dorothy, who was truly frightened to see the witch actually melting away like brown sugar before her very eyes.
Witch:	Didn't you know water would be the end of me?
Dorothy:	Of course not, how should I?
Witch:	Well, in a few minutes I shall be all melted, and you will have the castle to yourself. I have been wicked in my day, but I never thought a little girl like you would ever be able to melt me and end my wicked deeds!
Narrator #1:	With these words the witch fell down in a brown, melted, shapeless mass
Narrator #2:	And began to spread over the clean boards of the kitchen.
Both Narrators:	Eeeuw, gross!
Narrator #1:	Dorothy drew another bucket of water and threw it over the mess. Then she swept it all out the door.
Narrator #2:	After picking out the silver shoe
Narrator #1:	Which was all that was left of the old woman
Narrator #2:	She cleaned and dried it with a cloth
Both Narrators:	And put it on her foot again.

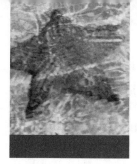

Skit with Narration

Why Do It?

Skits are another way for literature circles to bring their characters to life. The challenge in this project is, first, to pick a couple of high-interest scenes that someone who has not read the book can still relate to. Then students must write a script that includes some acting but also significant narration explaining the plot details and the characters so the audience understands what is going on. Note that this lesson requires two full class periods.

Teaching the Lesson

Getting Started

Start by having the groups choose a part of the book that has some action or conflict that other groups would find interesting.

Second, students must write a passage that introduces the book and the scene to the audience. Students need to decide which plot details need to be explained as well as what background is needed on the characters to be portrayed.

Third, students decide how they will perform their scenes, and then practice them. Groups have the choice of using pantomime as a narrator describes the action or giving the actors lines as well. Most groups choose a combination of the two.

Last, after the acting scenes are determined, the group must write a conclusion. Remind students that all of the group members need performance parts. No one gets to be the director!

The sample script from *White Fang* shown here includes all of the elements mentioned in the Getting Started steps. A group of boys put this script together. Of course, the scenes that most attracted them were the fight scenes—dog fighting, that is. The boys took great relish in portraying ravenous dogs and wolves, even including fake blood in one of their attack scenes. Ever thoughtful, the boys performed their skit on a bed sheet so that none of the blood would stain the new classroom carpeting.

Working the Room

Once students create their scripts, they need to unglue themselves from their seats and practice them. As you watch, help with the blocking. Kids always want to turn their backs to the audience when they're acting. Before the actual performances, have the groups work in pairs and take turns running through their skits in front of each other. In addition to giving the other group some feedback, this setup makes it easy for you to scan the entire room for on-task behavior. If the kids are following directions, you'll see one group performing and one group watching. If you see two groups sitting and chatting, it's time for a quick motivational intervention.

Reflecting

Any time you have performance project presentations, videotaping is a must. After the skits, have the kids watch the tapes and think about the following questions.

- What kinds of scenes really hold an audience's attention even though everyone hasn't read the book?

- What needs to be included in the script and narration so that the audience really understands what is going on?

- What were the best parts of my group's performance?

- Which parts of the performance didn't work out as well as we thought? What could we have done to avoid those problems?

After viewing the videotape, discuss the first two questions as a large group, making a master list of "good scene" characteristics and ways to help

Skit Script for *White Fang*

Narrator #1: Welcome, ladies and gentlemen, to Masterpiece Theater. Today we will be performing two selections from the classic tale *White Fang*. Let me provide you with some background information so that you will better appreciate our production.

Narrator #2: *White Fang*, written by Jack London, is a story of a wolf's struggle with nature. At the beginning of the story, a very cunning and equally sly She-Wolf gives birth to a very rambunctious and energetic pup. This pup, the only one in his litter to survive, becomes instantly fascinated by life. However, from the very beginning life is hard. Food is in short supply and White Fang's father is killed. White Fang is eventually taken from the wild and used as a fighting dog. Passed on from vicious master to vicious master, will life ever become easy for White Fang?

Narrator #3: Our first scene takes place early in the story. Two men, Bill and Henry, are on a journey across the frozen wild. Their journey is becoming more difficult as food is becoming scarce and, furthermore, a pack of wolves is following their trail. The wolves are thin and very hungry, so they have attacked the men's sled dogs.

Narrator #4: Frustrated, with only three bullets left, Bill loses his temper and takes off after White Fang's mother, She-Wolf, the leader of the pack. The character of Henry will be played by John and Bill will be played by Dave. The pack of wolves will be played by Tony and Joe.

Henry: No, Bill! You've got only but three bullets. Them dogs will eat you alive!

Bill: I won't stand for it. They ain't going to get any more of our dogs if I can help it.

Bill runs towards the wolf pack with his gun.

Henry: Say Bill, be careful. Don't take no chances!

Bill fires one shot and then two more. The wolves attack and take Bill down, eating their prey and howling at the moon.

Henry: Damn fool, never stood a chance. I warned him . . .

Soberly Henry carries on his way.

Narrator #1: This concludes the first half of our performance.

Narrator #2: Our second scene is towards the end of the novel. White Fang, now owned by Beauty Smith, is being used in dog fights. In this particular fight, White Fang's opponent is Cherokee, a bulldog owned by Tim Keenan. White Fang is extremely confused by this bulldog's fighting manner and doesn't attack as he normally would. We begin this scene as the fight is about to start.

Narrator #3: For this scene Tony will be playing White Fang, Joe will be Cherokee, John is Beauty Smith, and Dave is Tim Keenan.

Dogs are sitting in chairs at opposite corners like boxers as their owners/trainers encourage them to get out there and fight.

Tim: Come on Cherokee! Get him! You know what to do!

The gong sounds for the round and the dogs enter the ring. White Fang looks confused and circles Cherokee. Cherokee just sits and watches White Fang, taking little notice of him. White Fang attacks, tearing at the bulldog's shoulders but cannot get a hold on Cherokee's neck. Tim cheers his dog on, repeatedly. Beauty Smith just watches silently with a stern look on his face. Cherokee finally catches White Fang and knocks him off his feet. White Fang quickly recovers, but it is too late. Cherokee gets a grip on his lower neck. White Fang struggles to get the bulldog off, but because of the bulldog's grip on his windpipe, White Fang falls over, out of breath. Cherokee wins the match. Beauty Smith rushes into the ring and starts to beat the injured White Fang.

Narrator #1:   Will White Fang ever escape the vicious abuse of his masters? I hope we have in some way interested you in the story of one wolf's journey and the many obstacles he must face along the way. *White Fang* is a classic novel and is highly recommended by everyone in our book club group. *White Fang* can be interpreted many ways, but the basic idea is the same. The story represents a struggle through life. Be it through the eyes of a wolf or a man, life shall always remain a struggle inside the heart of any creature brave enough to live it.

Narrator #4:   This concludes our Masterpiece Theater performance. Thank you for your time. Goodnight!

---

the audience understand the book even if they haven't read it. (See the next figure for an example.)

Finally, have students return to their literature circles and discuss the other two questions. To wrap up, each group should prepare a self-evaluation that answers those two questions in depth. You might also have each student write a separate evaluation, indicating his or her specific contributions to the group project.

What Can Go Wrong?

As with the talk show project coming up next, you will see a wide range of quality in the skits. Encourage students to celebrate what worked well and analyze how to improve the next skit they do. Remember that getting better at performance is a key long-term goal: Kids are learning how to stand up in front of people, speak clearly with confidence, and remember what they're supposed to do. The nice thing about literature circle performance projects is that the students get to work in supportive small groups rather than stand up in front of the class all alone.

What Characteristics Make a Good Skit?

Script and Speaking

- Book and characters explained fully
- Each scene is set up for audience
- Said what the book was about
- Scenes were long enough so that you could tell what was happening
- Interesting, action parts of book chosen—major events of book
- Speak slowly and clearly
- Speak loudly—outside voice
- Setting is explained
- Speak with emotion, vary voice for different characters
- Lines memorized
- Lines well practiced—no stuttering
- Shows a lot of detail from the story
- Needs a conclusion, end of skit needs to make sense
- Gets people interested in reading the book

Acting

- Exciting scenes, lots of action versus standing still
- Used props
- Enthusiastic, energetic
- Good costumes
- No laughing—actors stay in character
- Prepared, well rehearsed
- Everyone in a scene can be seen— look at audience, don't turn your back
- Audience understands what the actors are portraying
- Make sure signs are big enough for the audience to read
- Exaggerate facial expressions
- Mix humor and seriousness
- Be realistic and act like you are really in the scene
- Acting should go along with narration
- Holds the audience's attention— entertaining—fun to watch
- End of skit leaves you thinking

Talk Show

Why Do It?

Talk shows are a staple of American culture. Instead of bemoaning the stupidity of the *Jerry Springer Show* and criticizing the smugly obvious answers of Dr. Phil, use these real-life caricatures to bring the fictional characters of your students' literature circle books to life. Sure, there's big-time comedy potential here, but placing characters in a new setting and giving them original dialogue also helps kids think about a novel in a deeper way.

Teaching the Lesson

Getting Started

Collect a few videotaped excerpts of the talk shows popular with your students. Rather than taping Jay Leno or David Letterman, it's actually better to stick with some of the more sensationalistic shows because the "larger than life" personas of the Springer/Phil ilk are easier to parody. These trashy shows also work well as models because they are usually themed; all of the guests have something in common. This format fits nicely with any novel since all of those characters definitely have something in common! Still, considering the often tawdry subject matter of these shows, be sure to screen for content as you select sample episodes for your class; "Life After Breast Enlargement" may not be where you want to go.

Tell the kids that they will be sharing their literature circle novels with the rest of the class via a talk show. As they watch the talk show excerpts, they need to think about the following questions:

- What kind of talk show would our novel's characters participate in?

- What would the theme be?

- How could the members in our group portray these characters? How would we talk? What would we say? How would we dress? How would we react to the other characters? What kind of personality would we reveal?

After viewing the show excerpts, have students meet in their book groups to brainstorm and begin writing a script. Give students some time each day to practice and plan; about fifteen minutes per class period tends to be just about right. Also, tell the groups that on the day of the performances they will have seven minutes from the time their group is called to the time they are cut off. Giving the time limit up front keeps the kids much more organized. If you don't, some groups will spend precious minutes on performance day figuring out where people are going to sit, arranging the chairs, and other details.

On the day of the performance, videotape the talk shows. Then students can use the tapes for self-evaluation when they reflect. Also, be sure to keep any really good examples as future models. Giving students a clear picture of what a high-quality project looks like automatically raises the bar and avoids confusion. After seeing an exemplary student performance, kids better understand the project and will work to make theirs as good as the one they saw.

Working the Room

Students generally have few problems coming up with a talk show idea and writing the script. They run into trouble with their portrayals of the characters. When the groups are given time to practice, you really need to roam the room and keep them on task. Kids tend to think that if they write the script, the rest of the performance will just miraculously happen. As you visit groups, make the members explain their characters to you. How will they enter? What clothing will convey that character? How will they act differently to show that character's personality rather than their own? Also, we've found it best to discourage students from attempting to use unfamiliar dialects. Though we don't think they intend any slurs, these attempts at accents sometimes contribute to ethnically insensitive, stereotypical portrayals. Besides, accents are hard to do. If Leonardo DiCaprio couldn't keep his Irish brogue going consistently in *Titanic*, your students are unlikely to succeed at mimicry either.

Reflecting

The day after the performances, run the videotape so the class can watch all of the projects. Have them take notes in their journals as they observe, keeping the following questions in mind:

- What makes a good talk show?

- What problems did a lot of the groups seem to have in common?

- What were the best parts of my group's performance?

- Which parts of the performance didn't work out as well as we thought? What could we have done to avoid those problems?

After viewing the videotape, discuss the first two questions as a large group, making a master list of good ideas and common problems. The next figure shows a list one class came up with.

Finally, have students return to their literature circles and discuss the other two questions. To wrap up, each group should prepare a self-evaluation that answers those two questions in depth. You might also have each student write a separate evaluation, indicating his or her specific contributions to the group project.

What Can Go Wrong?

Expect a wide range of quality in the talk shows. A few will be really good, most will be average, and a few may be torture to watch. This is typical when any project is attempted for the first time. The most important outcome is that students gain a better understanding of what needs to be done and then improve the next time.

What Makes a Good Talk Show?

Script and Speaking

- Speak slowly and clearly
- Host should give good description when introducing each guest
- Write script so that people who haven't read the book understand what's going on—give enough background info
- Audience can follow script easily
- Write script so that it covers the important parts of the book
- Speak loudly
- Rehearse lines—don't say um, like, you know
- Make sure host gives enough details so that audience understands what's going on
- Stress some words over others
- Characters should give their opinions, make a specific point
- Talk with enthusiasm
- Give a good summary of the book to get the audience interested
- Put emotion in voice; don't talk monotone
- End by giving the audience something to think about—doesn't just trail off

Acting

- Don't look bored—look excited, like you're having fun, give it some spunk
- Memorize your lines—don't stare down at your paper
- Talk and dress like the characters in the book—show character's personality—distinguish the characters so that the audience can tell them apart easily
- Get into character; don't play yourself
- Make the conversation sound casual, real
- Use lots of props
- Interact with the other characters—look interested in them—react to what they are saying
- Keep the audience interested—make it fun and interesting to watch so people will want to read the book
- Know when you are supposed to speak—act like you know what's going on
- Use humor when appropriate
- Look at the audience
- Sit up straight, don't fidget
- Act confident
- Use gestures and facial expressions
- Show some action—don't just sit there
- Use cue cards for audience

Jerry Springer Show **Script Based on** *The Great Gatsby*

The goal of this script was to illustrate Fitzgerald's underlying theme: Wealthy people play by different rules and use their money to smooth over problems. During the performance of this skit, the characters of Gatsby, Tom, and Daisy threw play money at each other to emphasize lines that had to do with their wealth or how they used money to influence others. It was very funny but also made their materialism and lack of morals clear.

Jerry: Today we have an interesting show planned for you that promises lies, backstabbing, and cheating on your spouse. This is what America is all about. I would like to introduce you to our four guests, who can be considered dear friends or bitter enemies. I would like you to meet Mr. Jay Gatsby, the main clown in this love circus.

Gatsby: How are you doing, old sport? How did you like my party last night?

Jerry: Sorry Gatsby, I didn't get an invitation!

Gatsby: Invitation? Come on, old sport! Everyone is always invited.

Jerry: I'll try to make the next one! Now I would like to introduce Daisy, the wife of Tom Buchanan. Rumor has it that Daisy and Gatsby are pretty close, if you know what I mean.

Daisy: Hi Jerry! How you doin' Gatsby? *(Daisy flirts with Gatsby.)*

Jerry: Whoa! That seemed like more than a friendly "hello" to me! Okay Gatsby, tell me about Daisy and yourself.

Gatsby: It started off in 1917, when I was an officer during the war. I saw Daisy and I immediately fell in love with her. I thought about her day and night, even when I traveled across the ocean to fight. It was five long years until I saw her again.

Daisy: I never thought I would see you again after you left the states to fight. I married Tom because he's rich and I guess he treats me okay!

Jerry: Rumor also has it that you are a little unhappy with your marriage.

Gatsby: Of course she is! She never loved Tom. She loved me all along.

Tom:	*(enters angrily)* Where is she? Where is she?
Jerry:	Well, as long as you are here, Tom, I might as well introduce you! Ladies and gentlemen, meet Daisy's despicable husband, Tom Buchanan.
Tom:	Where is that pretty boy Gatsby? *(Tom moves towards Gatsby, ready to start a fight.)*
Gatsby:	*(unfazed, standing up to shake Tom's hand)* How are you doing, old sport?
Daisy:	Boys, boys, boys! Let's try and settle this in a peaceful manner!
Gatsby:	Daisy, you can't say that you have seriously loved Tom, right?
Daisy:	Well . . . I do have a beautiful house, a wonderful daughter, a stable full of horses, and a swimming pool. Plus, the money isn't half bad!
Tom:	That is not what he asked you!!
Daisy:	Well, we do have a very nice view of Gatsby's house. Does that count?
Gatsby:	She has got you there, old sport.
Tom:	I have always loved you, Daisy, and I have never been unfaithful to you!
Jerry:	Hey Daisy, do you ever get strange phone calls from a lady whose name rhymes with turtle?
Tom:	Turtle . . . Myrtle?!?!?!?
Jerry:	Myrtle Wilson . . . Does that ring a bell?
Myrtle:	*(walking onto the stage)* Did someone call my name?
Jerry:	Well, the cat is out of the bag, Tom! If you were never unfaithful to Daisy, then I am the Easter Bunny!
Myrtle:	Tom, dear, what are you doing here? I was on my way to the dog groomer with Fluffy . . . remember the dog you gave me? Well, anyways, he needed a cut really bad. Then someone invited me to be on the *Jerry Springer Show,* but I don't know why.
Jerry:	Well, honey, you will in a minute!
Daisy:	Jay . . . Tom . . . who is this woman?
Myrtle:	Who are you? You look like you came out of a fashion magazine.

Daisy: *(strikes a pose and then walks towards Myrtle)* Well, you sure don't. Look at you holding on to that scrungy dog. I would say that you don't look all that bad for being a few pounds overweight.

Myrtle: *(getting in Daisy's face)* Boy you sure do sweat a lot! Do you have a gland problem? *(Myrtle and Daisy glare at each other)*

Tom: *(trying to sneak off stage)* Well Jerry, it has been great! I think I have a doctor's appointment in a few minutes!

Myrtle: *(Blocks Tom's exit, poking him in the chest as she talks to him; Daisy stands glaring at both of them.)* Tom, if you don't do some quick explaining, you are going to need more than a doctor, buddy!

Jerry: Alright! You all better sit down and let's do some serious talking. Put the dog down, Myrtle! Now what is honestly going on between you two?

Myrtle: I met Tom through my husband, George. He buys and sells cars and Tom was one of his customers. Tom took a liking towards me and I come up on the train to visit him sometimes.

Daisy: You what?!

Gatsby: Looks like you have been a pretty busy man, old sport!

Daisy: Tom, why are you even worried about me loving you? You don't even love me!

Tom: Of course I love you! I gave you that big, beautiful house, didn't I?

Myrtle: Yeah, you should be happy, Daisy. All I got was a crummy dog!

Gatsby: See Daisy, you shouldn't have married Tom. All you had to do was wait a little longer.

Daisy: How was I to know you bought a house in West Egg just to watch me from a distance? *(smiles flirtatiously at Gatsby)*

Tom: Gatsby, you are nothing but a creep! Spying on your neighbors?

Myrtle: Well Tom, you can't have it both ways! Either she goes or I go! Who is it going to be?

Jerry: Tom and Daisy, this must be the first time you have ever been honest with each other on this show or even in your whole life. Ladies and gentlemen, that is our show for today. Next week we'll be . . .

Gatsby: Party at my house! Bring your bathing suit; the pool hasn't been drained yet.

Jerry: Gatsby, are you going to mingle with the crowd for a change or hide like you always do?

Gatsby: Well, old sport, you will just have to be there and see.

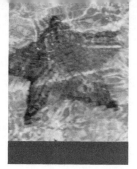

Brief the President

Why Do It?

We think that a balanced diet of reading, both for individuals and for book clubs, includes healthy servings of nonfiction. After all, 84 percent of the books bought and read in America are nonfiction. We're so passionate about this that Harvey and our colleague Steve Zemelman wrote a book called *Subjects Matter: Every Teacher's Guide to Content-Area Reading* (2004) to show how students can branch out into history, science, current events, mathematics, biography, adventure, memoir, self-help and all the other categories of nonfiction.

When kids read nonfiction trade books, they encounter facts, problems, theories, opinions, movements, debatable ideas, trends, arguments, and warnings. In short, many nonfiction books have policy implications. They confront us with important decisions or hard choices. When we read books like these, we want to do something, make a stand, take action, have some input. In the United States at least, the highest level of policy input would be to have some face time with the president—and that's just what happens in this activity, which we learned from Bob Ebersole and Bill Loris in Wheeling, Illinois.

Teaching the Lesson

Getting Started

Brief the President fits perfectly when your class book clubs have finished a set of nonfiction books with rich, current public policy implications. The following titles are some of our students' recent favorites:

The Future of Life, Edward O. Wilson

Fast Food Nation, Eric Schlosser

The Culture of Fear, Barry Glassner

Media Unlimited, Todd Gitlin

Food Fight, Kelly Brownell

Genome: Autobiography of a Species in 23 Chapters, Matt Ridley

Nickel and Dimed, Barbara Ehrenreich

All these books talk about highly charged, urgent, and timely social, political, or economic issues. Many take strong, partisan positions on the problems they detail and the prescriptions they recommend.

After kids have finished a book or just before the last scheduled club meeting, announce that they have an appointment at the White House, an opportunity to brief the president. Because the president is such a busy fellow, each group will have to pick one person to be the group's "briefer" (lobbyist, actually), and she'll get only five minutes to make the strongest possible case to the Big Guy. That means the group first needs to determine its position on the issues and create strong, clear talking points. Allow some work time (the better part of the class period) for groups to create a briefing paper (a script of bullet points) and to select and prep their briefer. Because the president or his aides may ask tough questions, it's important to anticipate contrary arguments of political resistance. The lobbyist must come in with:

1. a clear definition of the issue or problem

2. a strong opinion on the issue and a solution

3. research or facts backing up the opinion (citing the book, probably)

4. a specific requested action for the president to take

As groups prepare, they should also consider the decorum of the White House: how to address the president, how to be strong yet tactful, how to deal with aides, and so forth. And remember, lobbyists who come back empty-handed from opportunities like this don't remain employed for long!

When it's time for the White House meetings, you'll need a president and at least one aide. If you want to control things a bit and be sure that relevant, book-related questions get asked, you can play the president yourself. Or, to get the ball rolling and offer some modeling, you can play president for the first round but then recruit kids from other groups to take turns playing the president and his staff. Even if you model first, you'll still need to spend a few minutes clarifying these roles:

Lobbyist

1. Straighten your tie (metaphorically).

2. Act with some dignity.

3. Use formal language at the beginning of the meeting.

President

1. Be noncommittal at first. Every proposal can have negative political costs.

2. Be human and rational; if they have a case, you can say so.

3. Look at both sides of the issue; don't jump too fast.

4. Ask for facts, proofs, and specific details related to the proposed solution.

Aide

1. Show the lobbyist in and seat her/him near the president.

2. Always defer to the president, but you can ask really tough questions of the briefer.

3. Close off the meeting firmly but gracefully after *exactly* five minutes.

4. Feel free to improvise words or actions appropriate to the situation.

Working the Room

Your main job is to visit groups as they prepare their briefing points. The activity will work (and everyone will likely get some good laughs) as long as the lobbyists come in with a clear-cut "ask," a well-supported request for the president to take the public position or action recommended by the briefer. So as you circulate, make sure the talking points documents will get those jobs done. While the Brief the President meetings take place, you'll keep track of the time, move groups in and out, and help the "casts" switch places. This will be easier to do if you aren't the president yourself. Mainly, you can just sit back and enjoy the activity along with the kids.

Reflecting

The Brief the President meetings should be reviewed one at a time, as they occur. You can use the briefer's bullet list as a guide. (Did they define the issue? Did they explain their position?) Ask the class to discuss what arguments were effective and which ones flopped. Don't forget to solicit comments about the performance of the president and staff; you can use that feedback to guide the incoming group. The most important outcomes of any post-book project are to

1. help readers consolidate their thinking about the ideas and issues in the book and

2. get audience members interested in the books being portrayed.

Brief the President does a great job in both respects: It requires students to create a coherent "take" on the book, and it showcases tantalizing nonfiction for the rest of the kids.

What Can Go Wrong?

It is important that everyone take their parts seriously; if kids start goofing on the role of the president ("Give me some money, man, I'll support whatever you want . . ."), the substance is lost—although there may still be a lot of laughs. During one of our favorite Brief the President sessions, a persuasive lobbyist convinced the president that global warming was a left-wing plot. The alert kid playing the president's aide quickly mixed a pitcher of mock-martinis, and all the insiders toasted their commitment to ignore the "phony" issue of global warming.

chapter 10

Do It Yourself!

While reading this book, you have probably been wondering, "Can I design my own mini-lessons?" Or maybe you have been thinking, "Hey, I can create much better mini-lessons than these!" Well, please do! Indeed, we'd be perfectly happy if you just used ours as templates for developing your own, right from the start. The fact is, you'll have to create many of your lessons anyway, because your students will encounter problems or you may want to introduce skills that we haven't included here.

All forty-five lessons have a simple and consistent internal structure. As we've noted, there are two main types. Some lessons help the teacher introduce a new skill for students to practice while reading, taking notes, or meeting for discussion. The other variety aims to solve classroom-specific difficulties that arise in book clubs. Smart teachers develop their mini-lessons by observing the kids at work. They notice common problems, issues that several groups are struggling with (members coming unprepared, excessive digression from the book). They try to figure out what the next step is for these kids, and they shape these insights into mini-lessons.

The figure Two Types of Mini-Lessons shows the underlying structure we use to develop most mini-lessons. You'll notice that many of the steps are parallel, whether we are solving a problem or adding a new skill.

1. We focus on one clear topic, whether social, cognitive, or literary.

2. We explain why it is important and share how we have encountered the issue in our own adult reading life.

3. We enlist kids in defining the topic, issue, or problem.

4. We use short pieces of literature to practice the skill.

5. We ask kids to commit to applying the mini-lessons, and we put them to work immediately.

6. We always debrief afterwards: "How did today's mini-lesson work for you? And what shall we do next?"

For example, if you notice that many groups are drifting from their books into general conversation, you might plan a mini-lesson around this problem: "Over the past few days, I have noticed that many groups are having trouble staying close to their books." Next you'd explain why "orbiting closer to the book" is important, and maybe share a story of how you've seen adult groups suffer from digressing too widely. Then you enlist help: "Can anyone suggest ways we can deal with this?" As kids offer suggestions, make a list:

Put a note on the table in front of us: "Stick to the book!"

Remind each other to "orbit" near the book.

Videotape ourselves and watch how we are doing.

Use the egg timer and check ourselves every three minutes.

Invite a guest moderator.

Have one person be the on-task master.

Simply making this list is part of the solution; it visibly reminds students that they have a problem and need to deal with it.

Two Types of Mini-lessons

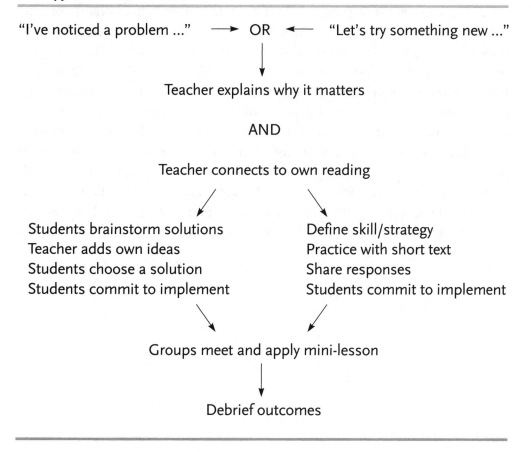

"I've noticed a problem ..." ⟶ OR ⟵ "Let's try something new ..."

Teacher explains why it matters

AND

Teacher connects to own reading

Students brainstorm solutions
Teacher adds own ideas
Students choose a solution
Students commit to implement

Define skill/strategy
Practice with short text
Share responses
Students commit to implement

Groups meet and apply mini-lesson

Debrief outcomes

Now it is time to choose an action step. The class can endorse a single solution, or individual groups can pick one they feel will work for them. Then give students a chance to practice their strategy on a very short piece of text: read, talk for three minutes, and then debrief. Or, you can simply send students straight off to their regular book clubs to put their solution to work during the day's meeting. When you regather as a whole class, ask students to reflect on how the chosen solution(s) worked. There are many formats for debriefing: Students might write individual journal entries, talk within their groups, or select a reporter from each group to share successes and problems.

One kind of mini-lesson is even simpler, requires little designing, and can have tremendous impact, especially if repeated often. That's when you, the teacher, simply talk for a few minutes about whatever you're reading right now, whether an adult or young readers' book. All you have to do is bring the book along and talk: Tell why you decided to read it, explain how the beginning worked for you, speculate on where the story seems to be going, describe how you're feeling about the book so far, explain how it connects to your life and other things you've read, and so on. Or read a passage aloud to share the author's style, humor, information, or language. This is teacher modeling in its purest form—a veteran book person "opening up her head" and showing kids how lifelong readers think and act. You can link your comments to the issues or problems you are seeing among your students, or just do it straight from the heart, as one of a thousand impressions that students need of lifelong literacy at work.

Appendix

Find Someone Who

Membership Grid

Book Pass Review Sheet

Abandoned Book Report

The Envelope, Please

Observation Sheet

Character Resumé

Video Reflections

Find Someone Who

Name _____

Date _____ Hour _____

Visited Another Country	Has a Favorite Spectator Sport
Has Favorite Pizza Toppings	Has a Favorite Junk Food
Likes Winter Weather—Why?	Went to See a Movie
Saw a Stage Play	Has a Favorite Book
Shops at a Favorite Store	Has a Favorite Restaurant
Has Siblings: #, Age, Gender	Is an Only Child—Advantages/Disadvantages
Hates a Vegetable	Loves a Vegetable

Membership Grid

Name _____

Date _____

Hour _____

Group Members					Topics

Book Pass Review Sheet

Name _____

Title:

Interest Rating:	Great 5	4	OK 3	2	Yuck 1
Difficulty:	Really Hard 5	4	3	2	Really Easy 1

Comments:

Title:

Interest Rating:	Great 5	4	OK 3	2	Yuck 1
Difficulty:	Really Hard 5	4	3	2	Really Easy 1

Comments:

Title:

Interest Rating:	Great 5	4	OK 3	2	Yuck 1
Difficulty:	Really Hard 5	4	3	2	Really Easy 1

Comments:

Title:

Interest Rating:	Great 5	4	OK 3	2	Yuck 1
Difficulty:	Really Hard 5	4	3	2	Really Easy 1

Comments:

Abandoned Book Report

Date:

Book Club Members:

Original selection:

Author:

Specific reasons for abandoning:

New selection(s):

Author(s):

Attach new reading and meeting schedule.

Signed:

_____

Members

The Envelope, Please...

Group Name _____

Date _____ Book Title _____

Mark down what page you are on right now _____ and the total book pages _____

Part I—Character

Based on what you've read so far, which character do you think will experience the greatest change by the end of the book? Think about changes in physical circumstances, lifestyle, relationships, or thinking/values. Describe what you think is going to happen to this character by the time the story is over. Briefly describe the clues in the story that make you think this.

Part II—In the End

Based on what you've read so far, how do you think the book will end? What problems will be resolved? What will happen to the main characters other than the one you discussed in Part I? Briefly describe the clues in the story that make you think this.

Observation Sheet

Name _____

Book Title _____ Date _____ Hour _____

Skills	Group Members				Total
Total					

Notes: Write down some specific things each member said that showed they were using one of the observed skills.

Character Resumé

Character Name _____

Book Title _____

The person I most admire is:

My favorite television program is:

One thing I do very well is:

If I had $100:

My favorite subject in school was:

Something I really want is:

Sometimes I worry about:

An important goal for me is:

Video Reflections

Group Members _____

Book _____ Date Taped _____

As we reviewed the tape, some strengths we noticed were:

Some areas that need improvement:

Specific plans/ideas we will implement at our next meeting:

Possible topics:

Being prepared	Using meeting time well	Sharing airtime
Asking good questions	Tying ideas to the book	Staying focused
Going deeper into ideas	Listening respectfully	Asking followup questions

References

Atwell, Nancie. 1998. *In the Middle: New Understandings About Writing, Reading, and Learning*. Portsmouth, NH: Heinemann.

Black, Lisa. "Students Face Discipline in Hazing Case." *Chicago Tribune*. May 6, 2003.

Calkins, Lucy. 2000. *The Art of Teaching Reading*. New York: Longman.

Daniels, Harvey. 2001. *Literature Circles: Voice and Choice in Book Clubs and Reading Groups*. 2nd ed. Portland, ME: Stenhouse.

Daniels, Harvey, Marilyn Bizar, and Steven Zemelman. 2000. *Rethinking High School: Best Practice in Teaching Learning and Leadership*. Portsmouth, NH: Heinemann.

Daniels, Harvey, and Marilyn Bizar. 1998. *Methods That Matter: Six Structures for Best Practice Classrooms*. Portland, ME: Stenhouse.

Daniels, Harvey, and Steven Zemelman. 2004. *Subjects Matter: Every Teacher's Guide to Content-Area Reading*. Portsmouth, NH: Heinemann.

Daniels, Harvey, Steven Zemelman, and Marilyn Bizar. 1999. "Whole Language Works: Sixty Years of Research." *Educational Leadership*, April.

Farr, Roger. 2004. "Guiding Students in the Think-Along Process," at <http://rogerfarr.com/mcr/taactivities/taactivities.html> (accessed March 2004).

Harvey, Stephanie, and Anne Goudvis. 2000. *Strategies That Work: Teaching Comprehension to Enhance Understanding*. Portland, ME: Stenhouse.

Harvey, Stephanie, and Anne Goudvis. 2001. *Strategy Instruction in Action* (video). Portland, ME: Stenhouse.

Hill, Bonnie Campbell, Nancy Johnson, and Katherine Schlick-Noe. 2000. *Literature Circles Resource Guide*. Norwood, MA: Christopher-Gordon.

Hill, Bonnie Campbell, Nancy Johnson, and Katherine Schlick-Noe. 1995. *Literature Circles and Response*. Norwood, MA: Christopher-Gordon.

Kagan, Spencer. 1994. *Cooperative Learning*. San Clemente, CA: Kagan Cooperative Learning.

Keene, Ellin, and Susan Zimmerman. 1997. *Mosaic of Thought*. Portsmouth, NH: Heinemann.

McMahon, Susan, Taffy Raphael, Virginia Goatley, and Laura Pardo. 1997. *The Book Club Connection*. New York: Teachers College Press.

National Assessment of Educational Progress. "Reading for Fun, Grade 4," at <http://nces.ed.gov/nationsreportcard/pdf/main2000/2001513.pdf> (accessed March 2004).

National Council of Teachers of English and the International Reading Association. *Standards for the English Language Arts*. 1996. Urbana, IL: NCTE/IRA.

Probst, Robert. 2004. *Response and Analysis.* 2nd ed. Portsmouth, NH: Heinemann.

Raphael, Taffy, Laura Pardo, and Kathy Highfield. 2002. *Book Club: A Literature-Based Curriculum.* Lawrence, MA: Small Planet Communications.

Rosenblatt, Louise. 1996. *Literature as Exploration.* 5th ed. New York: Modern Language Association of America.

Samway, Katherine Davies, and Gail Whang. 1996. *Literature Study Circles in a Multicultural Classroom.* Portland, ME: Stenhouse.

Schlick-Noe, Katherine, and Barbara Johnson. 1999. *Getting Started with Literature Circles.* Norwood, MA: Christopher-Gordon.

Short, Karen, Jerome Harste, and Carolyn Burke. 1995. *Creating Classrooms for Authors and Inquirers.* Portsmouth, NH: Heinemann.

Sierra-Perry, Martha. 1996. *Standards in Practice, Grades 3–5.* Urbana, IL: National Council of Teachers of English and the International Reading Association.

Steineke, Nancy. 2002. *Reading and Writing Together: Collaborative Literacy in Action.* Portsmouth, NH: Heinemann.

"Study Finds Rejection Is Literally a Huge Pain." *Chicago Tribune.* October 10, 2003.

Sweet, Anne Polselli. "A Research Program for Improving Reading Comprehension." In Sweet, Anne Polselli, and Catherine Snow. 2003. *Rethinking Reading Comprehension.* New York: Guildford.

Wilhelm, Jeff. 1997. *You Gotta BE the Book.* New York: Teachers College Press.

Zemelman, Steven, Harvey Daniels, and Marilyn Bizar. 1999. "Sixty Years of Research—But Who's Listening?" *Phi Delta Kappan,* March.

Zemelman, Steven, Harvey Daniels, and Arthur Hyde. 1998. *Best Practice: New Standards for Teaching and Learning in America's Schools.* Portsmouth, NH: Heinemann.

Literature Used in Mini-lessons

Anderson, Laurie Halse. *Fever 1793.*

Baum, Frank. *The Wonderful Wizard of Oz.*

Brooks, Kevin. *Martyn Pig.*

Brownell, Kelly. *Food Fight.*

Burdick, Eugene. *Fail-Safe.*

Collier, James Lincoln and Christopher Collier. *My Brother Sam Is Dead.*

Cormier, Robert. *The Chocolate War.*

Cornwell, Bernard. *Redcoat.*

Ehrenreich, Barbara. *Nickel and Dimed: On (Not) Getting by in America.*

Fitzgerald, F. Scott. *The Great Gatsby.*

Follett, Ken. *The Eye of the Needle.*

Forbes, Esther. *Johnny Tremain.*

Gitlin, Todd. *Media Unlimited.*

Glassner, Barry. *The Culture of Fear.*

Gobbell, John J. *The Last Lieutenant.*

Hickman, Homer H., Jr. *Rocket Boys.*

Hunt, Irene. *Across Five Aprils.*

Jakes, John. *The Bastard.*

Jakes, John. *North and South.*

Jakes, John. *The Rebels.*

Johnson, Charles. *Middle Passage.*

Klause, Annette Curtis. *The Silver Kiss.*

Lee, Harper. *To Kill a Mockingbird.*

London, Jack. *White Fang.*

Maruki, Toshi. *Hiroshima No Pika.*

O'Brien, Tim. *The Things They Carried.*

Paulsen, Gary. *The Winter Room.*

PEN/Faulkner Foundation, ed. *3 Minutes or Less: Life Lessons from America's Greatest Writers.*

Ridley, Matt. *Genome: Autobiography of a Species in 23 Chapters.*

Rinaldi, Anne. *Cast Two Shadows.*

Rinaldi, Anne. *The Fifth of March.*

Rinaldi, Anne. *Wolf by the Ears.*

Schlosser, Eric. *Fast Food Nation.*

Shaara, Jeff M. *Rise to Rebellion.*

Shakespeare, William. *Romeo and Juliet.*

Spinelli, Jerry. *Maniac McGee.*

Steinbeck, John. *The Grapes of Wrath.*

Steinbeck, John. *Of Mice and Men.*

Wilson, Edward O. *The Future of Life.*